# Teaching, Coach
# Adult Learners

The challenge for those coaching, mentoring, supervising or teaching adults is to design and deliver high-quality programmes that encompass a blend of teaching and learning approaches and strategies, that are constructed for adult learners in multiple educational environments and that cater for the diversity of adult learners' needs. Adult learners are complex individuals who come to the learning process with a multitude of different experiences. *Teaching, Coaching and Mentoring Adult Learners* helps practitioners step up to this challenge by developing the skills needed to share their expertise with adult learners and engage them in new transformative practices.

This book also forms a timely contribution to the current period of evolution in adult education, where extreme changes in the nature and scope of work and the globalisation of work and life are influencing learning. The shift in adult education addressed in this book includes:

- the globalisation of the workforce and the cultural impact on adult, tertiary and further education
- the relationship established between adult educators and adult learners
- provision of adult education and professional development by private and major multimedia and corporate interests
- occupations boundaries between professions and between skilled and unskilled work
- assessing adult learners' needs and adapting strategies to meet the perceived needs of adult learners in medicine, education, psychology and industry
- designing learning experiences to maximise the processing of complex conceptual knowledge and then transforming the knowledge to fit new learning environments
- the role of new technologies of learning in adult and vocational learning.

This book provides research-based insight into the expectations and the value of the coach, mentor, tutor and supervisor roles and combines research with strategic guidance to support the implementation of innovative techniques through case studies, strategies and methodologies in teaching and learning in higher education and professional learning. Bringing together insights from an expert range of international contributors, this text will be invaluable to higher education professionals and those involved in supervising, coaching and mentoring in the workforce.

**Heather Fehring** is Professor in the School of Education at RMIT University, Australia.

**Susan Rodrigues** is Professor in Science Education at Liverpool Hope University, UK.

# Teaching, Coaching and Mentoring Adult Learners

## Lessons for professionalism and partnership

Edited by Heather Fehring and Susan Rodrigues

LONDON AND NEW YORK

First published 2017
by Routledge
2 Park Square, Milton Park, Abingdon, Oxon OX14 4RN

and by Routledge
711 Third Avenue, New York, NY 10017

*Routledge is an imprint of the Taylor & Francis Group, an informa business*



*British Library Cataloguing in Publication Data*
A catalogue record for this book is available from the British Library

*Library of Congress Cataloging in Publication Data*
Names: Fehring, Heather, editor. | Rodrigues, Susan, editor.
Title: Teaching, coaching and mentoring adult learners / edited by Heather Fehring and Susan Rodrigues.
Description: Abingdon, Oxon : New York, NY : Routledge is an imprint of the Taylor & Francis Group, an Informa Business, [2017]
Identifiers: LCCN 2016010422 (print) | LCCN 2016022943 (ebook) | ISBN 9781138961043 (hbk : alk. paper) | ISBN 9781138961050 (pbk : alk. paper) | ISBN 9781315660028 (ebk)
Subjects: LCSH: Adult learning. | Mentoring in education.
Classification: LCC LC5225.L42 T43 2017 (print) | LCC LC5225.L42 (ebook) | DDC 374–dc23
LC record available at https://lccn.loc.gov/2016010422

ISBN: 978-1-138-96104-3 (hbk)
ISBN: 978-1-138-96105-0 (pbk)
ISBN: 978-1-315-66002-8 (ebk)

Typeset in Galliard
by Cenveo Publisher Services

# Contents

# Notes on contributors

**Owen Barden** (PhD) is a lecturer in Disability and Special Education Needs (SEN) at Liverpool Hope University, and a core member of Hope's Centre for Culture and Disability Studies. He previously ran an MA in Specific Learning Difficulties at Manchester Metropolitan University, a course for qualified teachers in the post-compulsory sector wanting to specialise in dyslexia tuition and study support. He has 14 years' experience as a teacher, lecturer and teacher-trainer in undergraduate and postgraduate Higher Education (HE), as well as Further Education (FE) and sixth form mainstream and SEN contexts.

**Valeria M. Cabello** (PhD) is an Associate Professor at the School of Education, Department of Pedagogy in Biology and Sciences, Universidad Central de Chile and a researcher at the Centre for Advanced Research in Education, Universidad de Chile. She began her career as an Educational Psychologist working in educational measurement, initial teacher education and adults' education in vulnerable contexts. Her interest in the psychology of adults' learning prompted her move to Scotland to pursue a PhD in Educational Psychology at the Centre for Peer Learning, University of Dundee. Her current main areas of interests are science teacher education and formative peer assessment of performance in higher education.

**Bulent Cavas** (PhD) is a staff member of the Dokuz Eylul University, Faculty of Education Department of Science Education, Turkey. During his graduate studies he worked as a research assistant at the Department of Science Education. He has joined 21 international and 14 national projects. He has over 100 national and international publications and written five books with department members. He has attended many international symposia, congresses and workshops in 30 different countries. His research interests are enquiry-based science education, teachers' usage of enquiry in their classrooms, ICT in science education, international comparative projects on science education, and the use of science labs. He was an executive committee member of IOSTE (International Organisation for Science and Technology Education) and organiser of the XIII. IOSTE Symposium on 'The use of science education for peace and sustainable development'. Dr. Cavas is President-Elect of ICASE (International Council of Associations of Science Education). He has served as an external expert for the European Union since 2009.

**Madawa Chandratilake** (MBBS, MMEd, PhD) is a Senior Lecturer in Medical Education, Faculty of Medicine, University of Kelaniya, Sri Lanka. He joined the Centre for Medical Education in September 2008 to carry out research activities and to contribute to the programme of courses in medical education. He graduated with his Master's degree in Medical Education from the University of Dundee in July 2008 gaining distinction. Madawa successfully completed his doctoral studies in January 2013. Madawa was a member of the academic staff in the Centre for six years and returned to his home in Sri Lanka to take up a senior appointment at the University of Kelaniya. He will, however, continue as an external tutor so the links with Dundee remain. His main areas of teaching include curriculum development, professionalism, assessment and clinical teaching. He has conducted medical education workshops both locally and internationally. He has been supervising master's projects carried out under a wide range of topics. He has several publications in leading medical education and clinical journals, and he has co-authored book chapters.

**Paul Edwards** is an experienced organisational change agent, with a background in strategic and management consulting, IT, and education (secondary and vocational). Edwards has worked throughout Australia and south-east Asia in over 36 organisations, where he brings about positive change through ensuring that employees want to move in the same direction as the organization. Most recently, Edwards has worked for a 'Big Four' Australian bank, where he was responsible for insourcing a critical business function across 32 countries and 30 regulatory jurisdictions. Edwards drove the change from business case to live operations in 18 weeks, leading to a 400% increase in quality of deliverables, a 60% reduction in cost, and a freshly energised department.

**Rita Ellul** (PhD) is a senior educator and consultant in the private sector in Australia, Rita leads a range of projects focused on school improvement and developing the capacity of school leaders. Dr. Ellul's career in education has spanned over 30 years and includes experience at school, regional and system levels. In these roles she has led school-based research projects into the use of new and emerging technologies and developed ICT professional learning for teachers and principals. Rita's PhD examined ICT peer coaching as a professional learning strategy to support teachers' integration of ICT into their teaching and learning programmes.

**Heather Fehring** (PhD) is a Professor in the School of Education in the College of Design and Social Context (DSC) at RMIT University. She has held the senior leadership roles of Director of Higher Degrees by Research in the DSC College and School of Education Deputy Head Research and Innovation. She was awarded the RMIT University Vice Chancellor's Distinguished Teaching Award in 2008 and in 2007 the Carrick Institute citation award for Australian University Teaching in the category of Outstanding Contribution to Student Learning: for a decade of sustained and significant contribution to students' and teachers' professional knowledge in the field of research and literacy education. Her field of expertise and publications are in the areas of teacher education, teachers' judgement and literacy assessment and from her ARC Linkage Grant (2006–2010) graduate workforce destination.

**Andrew Gibson** has extensive experience in solution focused coaching both as a BizFizz coach working with Business Owner/Managers, and as a programme manager for Enterprise Coaching projects on behalf of Bradford MDC and InCommunities Ltd. Andrew's previous experience includes: engineering, manufacturing and sales roles for Unilever plc; Business Unit Manager for Bass Brewers Ltd in the independent on-trade; creating a successful dot.com start-up for Bass Brewers Ltd in 2000 (www.barbox.com); and creating a successful web design company (www.easy-web-sites.co.uk). He has extensive and direct experience of the challenges of creating and running SMEs, including his own company, www.businessservicesleeds.co.uk. Andrew has applied solution focused practices to business, organisational and personal development for over seven years, and has delivered SF training workshops for businesses, charities and public sector clients.

**Carl Gibson** (PhD) has extensive experience in leadership roles in public, not-for-profit and corporate sectors and has worked in Europe, Asia-Pacific, Africa and North America. In his early career he served in both the British Army and the London Metropolitan Police, before undertaking a PhD, followed by postdoctoral research into a number of tropical viral diseases. His current research involves working with emergency services developing practical solutions to cognitive and decision-making issues experienced under extreme stress. He was a recipient of the 2013 Emergency Services Foundation Scholarship. As a result of this Scholarship he established a research programme with US federal firefighters looking at safety-related decision-making in wildfire operations and developed new operational concepts that have been applied in the USA and Australia. Carl has direct experience of leading high-performing teams in research, service delivery, and regulatory enforcement. He has served on a wide range of advisory boards and committees at national and international levels, including as the Head of the Australian delegation to the International Standards Organisation for Societal Security. He has also led a number of groups responsible for developing Standards in the areas of risk management and business disruption. He conducted numerous training and coaching workshops for a wide variety of organisations, including UK Cabinet Office, US Department of Homeland Security, and for a variety of agencies and companies in Australia, China, Thailand, Canada, UK, South Africa and New Zealand. Carl is currently a volunteer operational brigade officer and fire fighter with the Country Fire Authority as well as undertaking the role of Training Officer, designing and providing training to volunteer firefighters aged from 16 to 60 years old.

**Elizabeth Gibson** (PhD) initially trained as a chemist having obtained her BSc (Hons) Chemistry (Chelsea College) and PhD Physical Chemistry (Imperial College) from the University of London. She continued her research career as a British Gas Fellow and Phillips Fellow in the UK. She was also a volunteer police officer and a self-defence instructor with the London (Metropolitan) Police Force. Her first job on arrival in Australia was with Carlton and United Breweries where she became interested in management and leadership and was funded to undertake an MBA (Deakin University). Elizabeth then spent seven years in the Environment Protection Authority (Victoria) in a variety of senior management and executive roles. Two years were spent as State Manager of the Australian Government Analytical Laboratory where she managed 80 staff and a budget of $10 million. She spent three years as Executive Director of the Royal Australian Chemical Institute (the professional association for chemists) where she was successful in obtaining federal government grants to deliver chemistry education in schools. Elizabeth is now General Manager for CMPA (quarry association), which entails setting policy direction, spending time lobbying government on behalf of members and editor of the association magazine, *Sand & Stone*. She is also a volunteer operational member of the Country Fire Authority. Elizabeth has 50 publications ranging in topics from science through to management.

**Carolina Guzmán-Valenzuela** (PhD) is currently a researcher at the Center for Advanced Research in Education of the University of Chile, having previously been a Head of Department of Educational Psychology at the University of Valparaíso. She has conducted research as to the ways in which novice university teachers build their pedagogical knowledge and how reflective teaching practices might be promoted in the university. She is currently working on two topics: teaching practices in universities and how the link between teaching and research might be improved; and the conceptualisation of the contemporary university (specifically, the private–public debate), its interaction with neo-liberal regimes, and its impact on students' experience.

**Jack Holbrook** (PhD) is a visiting Professor at the University of Tartu, Estonia, with extensive experience in science education worldwide. His PhD is in chemistry, but he also has a school science teaching background, extensive experience in pre- and in-service teacher training; running in-service training workshops in a range of countries across Asia, Latin America, the Middle East and Africa, as well as in Europe. He is an education consultant in a range of Asian and African countries. His research covers curriculum development in science subjects, teacher education and assessment and evaluation as well supervising PhD students in use-inspired research, scientific literacy, enquiry learning and changing teacher beliefs. He has written and adapted numerous classroom teaching materials and published books for teachers as well as science textbooks for use in school. He worked as curriculum and assessment consultant for the Ministry of Education in Bangladesh (2009–2012) and from 2013 has been contracted by the World Bank for a curriculum project in Kuwait. He is the past president of ICASE and currently a member of the executive committee and heads the ICASE involvement in FP7 projects – PROFILES and ENGINEER.

**Richard Holme** is Lecturer in Education at the University of Dundee, Scotland. Richard began his teaching career as a primary school teacher, mainly working in middle and upper stages in the North East of England. He also held management responsibility for the technology and enterprise curriculum area. Richard completed his Master's degree in Education while still teaching, then entered initial teacher education. He is Admissions Convener on the MEd Programme and also Business Development Co-ordinator for the School of Education, Social Work and Community Education. His main areas of interests are primary maths, science and design technology education and professional learning and CPD.

**Deborah James** (PhD) graduated as a Speech and Language Therapist from University College London (UCL) in 1997. She completed her PhD in Psychology at UCL in 2002 where she studied the impact of cochlear implantation on young deaf children. She currently holds a readership in child and family communication in the Department of Social Work and Communities, in Health and Life Sciences at Northumbria University. She works practically and in a research paradigm to create new knowledge to bring change in families and workforces. Deborah is a practitioner, supervisor and trainer in Video Interaction Guidance. She is currently working with Children's Services at Newcastle City Council to develop the use of video feedback in social work for families who face complex challenges, with NHS England (North Region) to support workforce development in health visiting and with Northumbria Health Care Trust using video feedback to support reflexivity for staff working on wards for people with learning disabilities, autism and challenging behaviour.

**Celia McDonald** is employed as a Senior Rehabilitation Officer for blind and partially sighted adults in Liverpool as well as a Disability Access Auditor. The role of a Rehabilitation Officer for the Visually Impaired (ROVI) involves assessing individuals, identifying their strengths and weaknesses and creating and implementing a plan to achieve agreed goals. Currently working as the Senior ROVI, Celia is also responsible for the support and management of the Liverpool Rehabilitation Team. While working as a ROVI, Celia has also undertaken other duties such as: mentoring and supervising adult rehabilitation students on placement; Internal Verifier for Visual Impairment Awareness training (NVQ Level 2); External Examiner for Birmingham Central University Rehabilitation Studies Diploma course. She has also worked as an Architect (leading design teams) in the private and public sector and as a Voluntary Construction Worker and Team Leader, building houses for and with disabled native Canadians in remote parts of Canada. Celia's main focus at present is how visually impaired adults can be enabled to lead independent lives – whether through individual training, or advocacy regarding accessibility and increased awareness.

**Maureen Morriss** has spent over 25 years working with adults in education settings in Australia and the USA. She has been recognised for her work in developing, fostering and extending the professional learning of adults through a diversity of professional development opportunities. She has had extensive experience devising, delivering and evaluating programmes for regional, network, district and individual school use in one of the largest education systems in the world, New York City. She also works with, and alongside administrators, coaches and teachers to develop and strengthen the professional learning of these clients. Maureen's focused work has been predominantly in the areas of literacy development, curriculum design, assessment practices and data analysis informing instruction. She is currently the owner/operator of Maureen Morriss Consultancy Group LLC (MMCG).

**Hiroshi Nishigori** is an Associate Professor at the Center for Medical Education, Kyoto University, Japan. He graduated from Nagoya University School of Medicine in 1998 and became a Fellow of the Japanese Society of Internal Medicine (2004) and a Diplomate in Primary Care of the Japan Primary Care Association (2011). He obtained a Master's Degree in Medical Education from University of Dundee (2008). He is also working as an academic GP (General Practitioner) in the Department of General Medicine, Otowa Hospital, Kyoto. His research interests include BUSHIDO and medical professionalism (especially work ethics, altruism and pro-sociality) and Hypothesis-driven physical examination (HDPE), on both of which he published papers in international journals.

**Carey Normand** (PhD) is an independent educational consultant for Further Education (FE) and Higher Education (HE) in the UK. Formerly, Carey was Senior Lecturer in Education and Head of Learning and Teaching for the College of Arts and Social Sciences, University of Dundee (2004–2014). Carey's research interests and publications are in the spheres of professional learning and teaching, leadership and the policy–practice nexus in FE and HE; with a particular focus on the Scottish educational context. Her doctoral thesis examined conceptualisations of professionalism, professional identity and professional status for lecturers working in the College sector in Scotland. In 2013 Carey received £100,000 to support student transitions between FE and HE. Carey is currently editing a book on 'whole-mind' graduate attributes, for the twenty-first century.

**Miia Rannikmäe** (PhD) is a Professor and the Head of the Centre for Science Education and has considerable experience in science education in Estonia, Europe and worldwide (Fulbright fellow – University of Iowa, USA). She has a strong school teaching background, considerable experience in pre- and in-service teacher training and has strong links with science teacher associations worldwide. She was a member of the EC high level group associated with the publication of the 2004 report on 'Europe needs more scientists'. She is running a number of EC funded projects and is the grant holder for an Estonian research grant determining the change of levels of students' scientific literacy at gymnasium level. Recently completed grants were on modelling science education for relevance, an Estonian Science Foundation grant for exploring teachers' understanding of the Nature of Science, and Stakeholders' views on the goals of science education and its impact to students' career choices in science Her PhD students are involved in areas such as scientific literacy, relevance, creativity/reasoning, inquiry teaching/learning and the nature of science, stakeholders (incl. industrialists) interactions with the science education community. She has supervised three international postdoctoral students. She is a member of international research organisations ESERA, NARST, IOSTE and a member of the editorial board for several science education related journals (e.g. vice editor for the *Journal of Baltic Science Education*). She was the organiser of a 2010 ICASE & UNESCO World Science Education Conference on innovations in science and technology education and the organiser of the next Eurovariety conference in 2015. She is the past secretary for ICASE (International Council of Associations for Science Education) and is currently a member of the executive committee, chairing a standing committee for university liaison.

**Christine Redman** (PhD), Senior Lecturer in Science and Technology Education, heads the delivery of the Melbourne Graduate School of Education (MGSE) science education programmes in Australia. She is the inaugural Chair of the compulsory research subject that acts as a Capstone. Christine's research programme endeavours to make sense of relationships people have with each other, and when learning about, and using digital objects in their lives. Her research focuses on science education and ICT practices of teachers, students and academics. Christine has presented internationally on science education and innovative uses of technology. Her edited book, *Successful Science Education Practices* (Nova Publishers, 2013), disseminated contemporary research on quality science and technology education practices to practising teachers, teacher educators and pre-service teachers. In 2014 she completed three research projects that focused on iPads, IWBs and social media in educational settings. Currently she is on two research projects, both Australian federally funded Office of Learning and Teaching grants, focused on improving teaching practices in science education. One targets understanding the components of effective school-university based partnerships and the other, the use of scientists to support school-based teaching of science, technology, engineering and mathematics.

**Brian Rock** is a media research professional, with broad experience in media, marketing and advertising. His core expertise is working with complex data to find actionable insights to support sales and senior management, and developing the insights into clear evidence-based recommendations. He has worked in broadcast television, where he led a research project that resulted in a substantial overhaul of the network's business strategy, and has also worked in several creative and media agencies, as well as lecturing in advertising at the graduate and postgraduate level.

**Susan Rodrigues** (PhD) is a Professor in Science Education at Liverpool Hope University and Fellow of the Royal Society of Chemistry. She was also a Professor in Education at Northumbria University and Professor in Science Education Dundee University. She has held the post of Director of the Institute for Science Education in Scotland. She was a Director of Teacher Education for the Concurrent Teacher Education Programme at Stirling University. She has authored a number of publications for academic journals, technical reports, teacher guides and conferences. Her field of expertise is in the area of science education, teacher education and the use of technology in learning and teaching.

**Susie Schofield** (PhD) is a Senior Lecturer, academic lead for eLearning and internationalisation. Susie first joined the University of Dundee as a researcher / programmer on a European-funded eLearning project. She joined the Centre for Medical Education in 2006 as Staff Development Officer, working with NHS doctors involved in the delivery of the undergraduate medical curriculum. In 2009 she became Lecturer on the University of Dundee's Masters in Medical Education programme. With her expertise in pedagogy and online learning she was appointed eLearning academic lead, moving the Centre's paper-based distance learning course online. She continues to contribute to module development and teaching both online and face-to-face, and also as consultant to other potential programmes within the University. She created and leads modules in eLearning and faculty development for health professionals, and is particularly interested in the use of frameworks for continuing professional development, and their online support. As internationalisation lead in 2013 she works increasingly with faculties locally, nationally and globally, and has given numerous international keynote talks and workshops.

**Neil Taylor** is Associate Dean (Student Experience) at the University of Dundee, Scotland. Neil began his teaching career as a teacher of physics. He taught for several years and was Head of Department in a state school in Fife, Scotland. Neil was also a curriculum development officer at local authority level and national level for science education in the pupil age range of 5–14 years old. Neil then entered initial teacher education and was Programme Director for the PGDE (secondary) programme. His main areas of interests are physics education, primary science education, transition and eLearning.

**Greg Vinnicombe**, through his company Useful Conversations Ltd, has provided training for staff and consultancy for organisations in solution-focused practice for over 15 years. This included providing training for business coaches, as well as for staff and managers working with various service user groups in many public and third-sector organisations. For details see www.usefulconversations.com. Greg also provided NCFE accredited Level 3 Certificate and Level 4 Diploma courses in Solution-Focused Practice through a second company, Solution Focused Trainers Ltd.

**Eva Janice Youl** taught and managed Australian science education in country Victoria secondary colleges for many years. In 1997, as a Teacher Release to Industry recipient, she spent a year with the Research and Development Corporation, (RDC Dairy Australia). In 1998 Janice joined the Victorian Department of Education for a new initiative called Science in Schools. Janice then moved to curriculum and professional learning in Innovation and ICT and finally she developed digital resources for new arrivals and refugees. Janice is the director of Youl Education. She also continues to be an active community volunteer with schools, environment groups, the National Trust and Melbourne Museum.

**William Youl** began his career in scientific research and then moved into teaching science at a secondary college in country Victoria. This role included teaching Year 12 biology to adults in the evening. William then moved into the Technical and Further Education (TAFE) sector, teaching adult technicians from the food industry and also a range of subjects for a very multicultural local community. After 16 years of teaching, William moved into the food industry and management roles in quality assurance, safety and environment. The key to success in these roles is to be able to engage and influence the entire workforce. He is currently working with the dairy farming community across Australia to improve their people management skills on their farms.

# Introduction

## Adult educators working with adult learners

*Susan Rodrigues*

This book collates the expertise of adult educators working in tertiary institutions and/or workplace environments (media, health, finance, psychology, education, industry, and consultancy) around the globe with a view to considering the implications for professional development and professional learning in formal and informal interdisciplinary environments. Our book is research informed. But it is not intended to be a book that simply explores and reports on research on professional and adult learning. It is intended to be a book that allows those who were/are successful in their community of practice to share what they know and understand with other adult educators working with adult learners in a variety of settings. The book is intended to help those working with adult learners to navigate through institutional, strategic and personal perspectives in order to address the challenges and opportunities they encounter in their work with adult learners.

This book brings together expertise derived from a variety of interdisciplinary fields in which adult learners are supervised, taught, coached or mentored. We present broad theoretical and practical perspectives to better inform coaches, mentors, supervisors and teachers engaging with adult learners at different levels and in formal and informal contexts. The world now demands a work force that is globally mobile. Thus courses and professional development aimed at adult learners has to meet the needs of these international demands. Consequently, providing professional education for adult learners must cater for diversity, cultural competency and international quality assurance expectations. The book provides an insight into the expectations, the distinctiveness and the value of the coach, mentor, tutor, and supervisor role in formal and informal environments involving adult learning.

The various chapters in this book address interdisciplinary aspects of the wider context of adult learning. The chapters consider professional development in terms of mentoring, coaching, teaching and supervising within different milieus and from different perspectives. They present research evidence in tandem with authentic concrete examples in order to encourage adult educators to reflect on practice and develop informed strategies. Each chapter ends with a provocation. These provocations are intended to help the reader evaluate and inform her/his role, as coach, mentor, teacher or supervisor.

## Defining mentoring, coaching, teaching and supervising

Mentoring tends to be used in circumstances that involve a more experienced person working with a protégé. It tends to be a relationship that is long term and intended to foster the mentee's professional or academic or personal development. Mentoring can involve one to one, or a network of mentors or a peer group (Davis, 2001). The relationship between a mentor and mentee can be formal or informal, long or short term, face to face or via distance (Packard, 2003).

Some suggest that Socrates was a coach because the Socratic method involves asking a series of questions that lead one to examine assumptions and change views. However it was Sir John Whitmore who introduced Coaching for Performance in the UK in the 1990s that saw coaching establish itself in the business world. Coaching is thought to operate on two levels: transactional and transformational. The transactional level could be described in terms of moving furniture around in your home or redecorating your home, whereas transformational would be selling your home and relocating! Definitions for coaching range from a coach motivating a coachee to help them to do their best, to a coach's skill in helping a coachee develop specific areas of their performance or skill.

Teaching tends to be used as a relatively sweeping term to describe any activity or practice which results in someone acquiring skills and knowledge. It is often used with specific reference to an educational setting, but in reality it applies in formal and informal environments. The nature of tutoring is quite difficult to define for it means many things to many people. But in general it tends to be associated with a teacher and/or someone with a more didactic role.

Supervision tends to be seen in terms of overseeing a process during the execution of that process. Someone in the role of a supervisor tends to have oversight of another person's engagement with a particular task or action. Interestingly, supervising PhD candidates warrant supervisors with both an oversight and a capacity to gradually relinquish their role as expert as the candidate adds a new body of knowledge and becomes in essence an expert in her/his area.

At a superficial level, coaching tends to be seen as short term and intended to suit a given task, whereas mentoring involves a longer relationship between the mentor and mentee. In addition, it could be argued that a coach is more likely to determine the goals, help prescribe task-related skills and identify performance expectations. In contrast, a mentor is a supportive facilitator where direction and progress is co-determined by the mentee and mentor. Mentoring and coaching are professional learning strategies that focus directly on the needs of the learner. Mentees and those being coached actively identify their learning needs and direct their learning agenda with the support of their mentor or coach. A supervisor probably starts with more of a coaching role and ends with more of a mentoring role as the person being supervised acquires skills and knowledge that may in some cases take her/him beyond the scope of her/his supervisor. Teachers, in the broadest sense, will attempt to share knowledge and skills in the belief that their strategies result in another increasing their knowledge or skill base.

## Organisation of chapters

In this book, as previously stated, each chapter concludes with a provocation. The aim of the provocation is to foster reader reflection to guide and inform practice. While the chapters draw on research evidence they are not meant to be simply an exercise in presenting a topic overview. The research perspective is presented alongside practical reality in order to substantiate the mooted approach and guidance. As the chapters are intended to help those who work with adults and have the role of mentor, coach, supervisor or teacher, we hope the provocation will link theory to practice and practice to theory.

The first four chapters focus on the adult educator. The aim is to help you, as an adult educator, in terms of reflecting on and developing your professional identity and professional development. As such, this first batch of chapters focus on helping you as an adult educator to think about what you understand by the terms (coach, mentor, tutor, supervisor) before you look at your professional identity formation, your ability to reflect on practice and your understanding of professional development.

The next batch of four chapters encourages you as an adult educator to consider the perspective of your adult learners and to examine the factors that affect or influence your adult education practices. As such, this batch includes chapters that encourage you to consider the adult learner's cultural diversity, special educational needs (specifically sight impairment), language and communication strategies and technology landscape.

The final section of three chapters contains what are case studies in essence. They draw and reflect heavily on practical implementation in a variety of contexts. There is, for example, a chapter written by three authors working in finance, media and the chemical industry, and they describe best and worst case managerial strategies. Another chapter was written by two coaching consultants and they show how their strategies could help other adult educators change practice. The final case study chapter is written by international science teacher educators who offer vignettes and describe strategies they used to promote teacher education.

## An overview of each chapter

In this book most of the chapter authors use the term adult educator to refer to the coach, mentor, tutor, and supervisor. We also use the term adult learner to represent the adults who may be coached, mentored, supervised or taught.

In Chapter 1, Rita Ellul (an education consultant in the private sector in Australia) and Heather Fehring (a Professor in the School of Education, College of Design and Social Context at RMIT University) highlight some of the key features of the distinction between coaching and mentoring practices. They describe the essential professional development strategies needed when teaching or supervising adult learners. Developing appropriate learning opportunities, which address any content requirements, need to be underpinned by pedagogical approaches, which take into account both the professional and personal needs of the adult learners. The chapter provides research-based evidence and considers the implications of this evidence when it comes to implementing coaching and mentoring that focus on adults' professional and personal development beyond 'cold cognition'. Ellul and Fehring suggest that astute, strategic thinking is required in order to identify professional learning that aligns best with adult learning principles and the identified needs of learners to make a positive impact on their learning. These assumptions can be used by you as an adult educator to inform the way in which you structure professional learning to optimise meaningful engagement by your adult learners. The process commences with the adult educator establishing a positive climate for learning. It advocates a collaborative approach between the adult educator and adult learner. It also highlights requirement elements such as mutual planning, identifying the needs for learning, developing the programme objectives, designing the learning experiences, evaluating the learning outcomes and identifying new needs to inform the next cycle.

In their provocation, Ellul and Fehring look at effective and efficient mentoring or peer coaching practice that facilitate the needs of the adult learner and the nature of the professional development activity. This includes designing professional development after ascertaining the prior experiences and the background of the adult learners. It also includes considering how to structure occasions for peer coaches to work together at different stages to share effective practices. Ellul and Fehring suggest adopting an approach where mentoring occurs between an experienced member and new member, where the experienced member is an expert resource providing collegial support. Some adult educators might see this as a zone of proximal development approach (Vygotsky, 1998). Peer coaches are able to work collaboratively to improve an area of need identified by the coachee, and similarly to the role of mentee, with the coachee actively defining and directing his/her learning experience. The sample coaching questions demonstrate a range of clarifying and open-ended questions through which a coach could facilitate a conversation. Embedding mentoring and/or coaching in the culture of the respective environment requires commitment to the careful matching of mentoring and coaching pairs in order to optimise the potential for success. It also requires time for mentoring and coaching pairs to meet formally and it requires procedures or guidelines, which set out the expectations and responsibilities of all participants. Ellul and Fehring suggest that if you are planning a peer coaching programme you need to consider how you could structure opportunities for the peer coaches to work together in a collegiate, interactive and mutually supportive learning context at different stages to share and embed effective coaching practices.

In the second chapter Carey Normand (an independent consultant for Further and Higher Education in the UK) and Maureen Morriss (with over 25 years of experience working with adults in education settings in the USA) explore the concept of professional identity. They consider the literature on professional identity and professionalism. Following this they supply and discuss strategies, approaches and techniques in support of the formation of professional identity. The Beijaard, Meijer and Verloop (2004) literature review on teachers' professional identity found that there was no clear definition of professional identity. From this review, the authors concluded that there were 'four essential features of teachers' professional identity': first, that it was an 'ongoing process' that was dynamic and not 'stable or fixed'; secondly, that it constituted both the 'person and context' and, therefore, illustrated that people will behave differently in different contexts based on their own value base and 'own teaching culture'; thirdly, that 'sub-identities' make up the 'teacher's professional identity', again linked to the person, experience and to her/his relationships within a context; and fourthly, that teachers are active engagers in the process of 'professional identity formation' and it is not so much about what they have but about how they use this 'to make sense of themselves as teachers' (Beijaard et al., 2004, pp. 122–3).

Normand and Morriss suggest that there is unlikely to be one identity but rather there will be a multiplicity of identities that reflect personal contexts. So professional identity is socially situated within occupational groups and understood relationally (for example, between individuals and groups and organisations). In their chapter Normand and Morriss use two main contexts to provide examples of the ways in which professional identity can be fostered. Normand and Morriss also identify the need to understand and recognise what is of key importance to you, as the professional, and to prioritise those elements. But they also suggest that it is wise to use your skills to benefit the workplace first. Normand and Morriss have a straightforward provocation in their chapter. They suggest that you ask yourself what you would want professional contemporaries to say about you when you are not present.

In the third chapter Carolina Guzmán-Valenzuela (with her prior experience as Head of Department of Educational Psychology in Chile) and Valeria Cabello (with her prior experience as an Educational Psychologist working with adults' in vulnerable contexts in Chile) examine the concept of reflective practices by revisiting the work of Donald Schön. Schön's ideas around the reflective practitioner and 'the epistemology of practice' (Schön, 1983) led in the 1980s to much examination regarding reflective practices across disciplines and at different education levels. Guzmán-Valenzuela and Cabello go beyond Schön's (1983, 1987) ideas about reflective practices in diverse professional settings by stressing the importance of enhancing professional reflection systematically through collaboration. The Guzmán-Valenzuela and Cabello chapter explores research and practice in adult education in terms of communication, behaviour, attitude and practice. It considers professional resilience and professional learning from the viewpoint of the adult educator and the adult learner. The chapter considers how to achieve effective multi-agency work that builds an environment, language and ethos able to adapt to the practices of others with wide ranging professional and community agendas. Reflection on action is a retrospective action (McAlpine et al., 1999) that gives space and time to professionals to re-construct their professional actions, re-analyse the explanations generated around a problem and consider the strategies used in order to solve it. The provocation in this chapter includes keeping shared journals in which the adult learner sets and documents realistic goals. The adult learner will also use the journal to identify progress during supervision meetings and keep a note of their progress in the journals. Guzmán-Valenzuela and Cabello suggest spending time during the supervisory relationship to address the necessary and challenging elements that arise during the intervening periods. They also suggest the journals should be accessible to the supervisors. Guzmán-Valenzuela and Cabello also advocate a zone of proximal development (Vygotsky, 1998) element by suggesting that the adult learner and supervisor write a short article about their professional learning experience that identifies strengths and weakness. In their chapter Guzmán-Valenzuela and Cabello make a case for why professionals need to use an amalgam of knowledge drawn from both disciplinary frameworks acquired by formal education and from their own professional experience. For while acquiring disciplinary knowledge is basic when starting a professional life, practical knowledge embedded in situated practices in particular professional milieus helps to adapt, modify and create new knowledge. This is particularly important when a professional dilemma appears and when a solution can be found neither in disciplinary knowledge nor in prior similar situations. In those circumstances, the professional might find that her/his capabilities are inadequate. So s/he will search for and assimilate relevant formal propositional knowledge and/or will try to acquire systematically relevant new skills and/or new understandings in order to address a difficulty. As a consequence, it is important that you as an adult educator are conscious of your own actions. You need to be capable of detecting when a problem or a challenge arises and make explicit your implicit knowledge in order to redirect your actions to new possible solutions or courses of action. In order to promote professional learning through reflection, adult educators should aim to develop activities such as writing reflective journals, conducting group projects and case studies, and performing roleplay and simulations. It might be worthwhile from time to time to organise a collective supervision with other adult learners and adult educators. This might encourage sharing learning goals and triangulating perspectives around challenging situations or strategies to address unexpected problems.

In the fourth chapter Carl Gibson (who has conducted coaching workshops for a wide variety of organisations, including UK Cabinet Office, US Department of Homeland Security, and agencies and companies including training volunteer firefighters in Australia), Richard Holme (a teacher educator) and Neil Taylor (an Associate Dean (Student Experience) at the University of Dundee) consider what might be effective professional development in terms of learning, memory and intuition. Their chapter provides an overview of what might constitute the notion of professionalism in education and looks at models of professionalism and models of professional development. The chapter discusses how to plan and execute effective professional development (including developing shared sense making). Their chapter also considers operational aspects (resources, planning, structural, risk). Risks to executing effective professional development include the effect of heuristics and biases. The Gibson, Holme and Taylor chapter advocates reflecting on the challenges posed when considering a personal issue and the conflicts that may arise as a consequence of individual/institutional philosophy, religion or politics. This chapter also includes a section on neuroscience, based on the argument that the design and delivery of professional development programmes can benefit when based upon an understanding of the strengths and weaknesses of the human brain. Thus Gibson, Holme and Taylor describe a 'brain-based' model of professional development. The chapter describes a range of techniques an adult educator can use to help learners maintain attention. Their chapter gives adult educators a chance to use these models to analyse their professionalism and approaches to professional development.

In the fifth chapter, Owen Barden (a lecturer in Disability and Special Education Needs at Liverpool Hope University), William Youl (currently working with the dairy farming community in Australia to improve their people management skills on their farms) and Eva Youl (who has recent experience in developing digital resources for refugees in Australia) look at cultural aspects of inclusive education. There is no easy or universally agreed definition of 'inclusion'. However, one way of thinking about the concept is in terms of attempting to make education accessible and meaningful for all, with everybody learning together with and from each other (Hart et al., 2004). There has always been a pragmatic motivation for inclusion. Countries have adapted their education systems in response to increased socio-cultural diversity, greater labour-force mobility and in an attempt to try and promote social cohesion as well as economic productivity (Armstrong et al., 2010). Barden, Youl and Youl present evidence of adult learners' educational experiences, and use it to show that it is imperative that adult educators understand the cultural backgrounds of their adult learners when striving to provide inclusive education. Adult learners who are disabled, who are educationally or economically disadvantaged, or who are immigrants (and some adult learners will be all three) can often be frustrated in their attempts to participate in continuing education because they are made to feel different and inadequate by their peers and adult educators. The adult learners may also lack the information and support they need to be successful. They may struggle financially, or may not understand what their educators or institutions want from them. Barden, Youl and Youl interviewed adult learners and their educators to try and get a sense of their personal, family and community backgrounds, what they perceived as the barriers to inclusive education, as well as their ideas of what made for good educational practice. The adult learner voices in the Barden, Youl and Youl chapter provide insights that you as an adult educator might need to take into consideration. Barden, Youl and Youl identify the importance of adult educators prioritising inclusive thinking in reflection and practice. The adult learner voices in this chapter indicate four themes: motivation (to further their careers, to increase their salary, to find a new career, to improve themselves, for recognition); obstacles (language difficulties, financial struggles and competing demands); learning preferences (equitable design, flexibility, simplicity, formative feedback, learning communities); and what makes a good educator (knowledgeable and enthusiastic about their area of expertise, patient, focus on the positives, student-led sessions). The authors suggest that as well as adult educators recognising their role in adult learners' support networks, adult educators can maximise learning opportunities by following the principles of Universal Design for Learning (UDL). After all, generally speaking, providing more pathways to learning by providing information in different formats helps everybody learn better. So, as well as adult educators taking the time to get to know their adult learners, UDL can help take account of cultural diversity as well as individual strengths, preferences and challenges. You as an adult educator could capitalise on adult learner motivation by creating inclusive environments that are active, engaging and effective for all. Barden, Youl and Youl complete their chapter with a provocation in the form of a checklist to use when considering adult learners from diverse cultural backgrounds.

The sixth chapter by Celia McDonald (with her experience as an Architect leading design teams including building houses for and with disabled native Canadians in remote parts of Canada and more recently as a rehabilitation officer and project officer at Liverpool Hope University) and Susan Rodrigues (a Professor in Science Education at Liverpool Hope University) focuses on the experience of teaching visually impaired adults. Their chapter considers the following aspects: how to communicate, bearing in mind there are limited or no visual cues; the physical layout of the learning environment including lighting; accessible information; timing of presentation of information; the importance of monitoring, recapping and reviewing; teaching within groups and different subjects; services and resources available and how to find them. The authors identify issues that an adult educator might sometimes overlook. For example, it is worth bearing in mind that it is not possible to skim read when reading Braille, which can take up to three times as long as other learners reading text, or if the person has a special computer with the translated text available. The chapter includes examples/scenarios from McDonald's experiences as a Rehabilitation Officer. McDonald and Rodrigues suggest that when working with a visually impaired person, preparation should include what was identified in an assessment. The exchange model of assessment is not just a process of asking a list of questions. It is observing adult learners' behaviour, listening to what they say (not just in response to the questions), and discussing with the adult learners their strengths and difficulties and the reasons for these strengths and difficulties, as well as identifying past experiences (good and bad). As an adult educator you will have to ascertain the availability of resources as well as who is responsible for providing particular materials (Braille, large print, support worker, specialist computer). As indicated in the section in this chapter on misconceptions, while the other senses may not compensate for sight loss, a well-prepared adult educator will have assessed the limitations, or preferences of the visually impaired adult learner. The McDonald and Rodrigues provocation involves the JKLMNO approach: Justification, Know, Learning, Match, Needs, Objectives.

In the seventh chapter by Susie Schofield (a Senior Lecturer and academic lead for eLearning and internationalisation at the Centre for Medical Education, University of Dundee), Madawa Chandratilake (a Senior Lecturer in Medical Education, Faculty of Medicine, University of Kelaniya, Sri Lanka) and Hiroshi Nishigori (an Associate Professor at the Center for Medical Education, Kyoto University, Japan) look specifically at how technology is currently used in the teaching and supervision of medical students and trainees in the UK, Sri Lanka and Japan. Each country has a different training structure, culture and level of technology immersion of its students, teachers, health practitioners and patients. Each of these has implications for how technology is used and how it might be further exploited in a way acceptable to key stakeholders. What is universal though is the ultimate aim of any medical training – to benefit the patient. Schofield, Chandratilake and Nishigori signal an increasing interest in the flipped classroom where medical students review lectures online and the traditional face-to-face lecture time is used for more active learning. They also suggest there is an increasing interest in use of mobile technology on the ward with evidence of the use of mobile devices for educational and patient care purposes occurring in all settings, from the classroom to the hospital. Schofield, Chandratilake and Nishigori, suggest that adult learners use mobile devices mainly for information management, communication and time management while 'on the go'. However, it would appear that in Sri Lanka, although m-learning has been experimented with and used as a part of formal curriculum in other fields it is rare in medical education. In the UK, facets like a quiz within the virtual learning environment, or at the start of a session via an audience response system or one using students' own mobile devices allow for responses (which may be named or anonymous). Schofield, Chandratilake and Nishigori suggest that UK undergraduate courses have moved from the written open-question exam, long case and viva voce to MCQs (multiple choice questions), EMIs (extended matching items), OSCEs (objective structured clinical examinations), portfolios (increasingly online) and simulations, and at trainee level case-based discussions, mini clinical evaluation exercises, direct observations of procedural skills and mini peer-assessment tools. As such, an adult educator working in the medical education field faces a challenging learning curve when it comes to the use of technology in the teaching and supervision of medical students and trainees.

In the eighth chapter Christine Redman (a Senior Lecturer in Science and Technology Education at Melbourne University) and Deborah James (a Reader in Child and Family Communication in the Department of Social Work and Communities, at Northumbria University) report on, and explain, the background thinking that precedes planning for a relationship with adults in different settings. The chapter details theoretical concepts that underpin developing and maintaining positive and effective communication strategies for strong learning relationships. One of the points made by Redman and James is that at any site (be it a workplace or education environment), over any period of time, practices are established. These practices become refined, and are adopted, imitated, reproduced and transferred. Eventually these practices are so ingrained in situ that they are no longer up for discussion. These practices become tacit and rarely contested or re-examined. Redman and James suggest that little change will occur if adult educators do not know which assumptions inform their expectations, and consequently do not know why they do what they do. As a consequence Redman and James suggest that you as an adult educator need to identify your assumptions about what you do as this can help you to understand, examine and change tacit assumptions that actively underpin reflected habits.

They suggest that it is important to re-position to consider the importance of the changes, and second to re-position towards a feeling of confidence and commitment so that as a community there is a collective sense that the adult educator and adult learners have a shared vision with which to inform their perception of the changes. They describe strategies such as 'collaborative interactive discussions' and 'personal meaning making maps' that an adult educator could use to foster adult learner curiosity in and about their current work practices.

In their chapter Redman and James provide examples to show how to support adult learners (but the same would apply to adult educators) to encourage them to consider modifying their existing practices. There is a certain amount of risk taking if clinicians and teachers are to replace established practices with new practices that warrant time to refine them. Redman and James highlight the need for time to be spent on approaches that make clear or develop underlying principles. These drivers would help ensure that those involved understand the impetus for changes in the environment as well as better understand the adult learner, and consequently have a chance to develop both a personal and a collegiate motivation to attend to these changes in the milieu.

The ninth chapter by Paul Edwards (an organizational change agent, with a background in strategic and management consulting and most recently working for an Australian Bank), Brian Rock (a media research professional, with experience in broadcast television, media, marketing and advertising) and Elizabeth Gibson (who trained as a chemist and was the Executive Director of the Royal Australian Chemical Institute and is now General Manager for a quarry association) is the first in the case study series. Edwards, Rock and Gibson look at what it means in a practical sense to be a leader and a mentor. Focusing around lessons learned from practical experience rather than leadership theory, Edwards, Rock and Gibson present three distinct case studies that identify useful techniques to apply and pitfalls to avoid. The mini case studies in this case study chapter provide a problem statement, which sets the scene and context. The first two mini case studies within this chapter include a description of an approach taken to solve particular issues, and describe the relatively positive outcomes achieved as a consequence of the approach. The third mini case study in the chapter, in contrast to a positive working environment, describes dealing with a situation where a team manager is unable or unwilling to provide clear, firm, and decisive leadership. Thus the three mini case studies outline positive and negative strategies that were used. Edwards, Rock and Gibson report on positive principles that adult educators should take on board when leading teams: establish and communicate clear objectives, provide as much direction as needed to enable team members to deliver on these, and reinforce positives. But Edwards, Rock and Gibson also highlight strategies that are likely to have negative outcomes. For example they do not advocate starting a discussion about a project with the words 'as usual I expect you've done nothing about it' as this is unlikely to empower people!

Andrew Gibson and Greg Vinnicombe wrote the tenth chapter which is a case study chapter. Sadly, soon after submitting this chapter for penultimate review, Greg Vinnicombe died in a road traffic accident.

In the tenth chapter Gibson (an experienced Solution Focused Coach with previous experience working for Unilever and Bass Brewers) and Vinnicombe (who used to provide training for business coaches, as well as for staff and managers) describe a strengths-based coaching model called Solution Focused Practice (SFP) that helps people to identify their aims and objectives for a given situation. They show how SFP can be used to identify and make progress towards specific goals. The technique focuses on the interactions between people and on the desired future state of the people involved. Where traditional teaching relies on the expert knowledge of the adult educator and the willingness of the adult learners to learn from this knowledge, SFP assumes that at times while the adult educator (coach) may have some important professional knowledge, the adult learners (clients) have most or all of the knowledge and resources required within themselves and their network to put the knowledge relevant to their circumstances into practice. Having explored what clients want, the differences they seek, and the abilities and resources they can build on, the coach would now have the opportunity to explore what would be different if a small step was taken towards the desired future state. Their experience over several years of applying SFP has demonstrated that by applying this process and spending as little time as possible on analysing the deficits to be overcome (the problems, barriers, things that are going wrong and not wanted), their clients usually start to make progress towards their desired outcomes and the deficits identified reduce in impact, and often disappear altogether.

In the eleventh chapter Miia Rannikmäe (Professor and the Head of the Centre for Science Education), Jack Holbrook (a visiting Professor at the University of Tartu and an education consultant in a range of Asian and African countries) and Bulent Cavas (a staff member of the Dokuz Eylul University, Turkey and President-Elect of the International Council of Associations of Science Education) use the context of teaching science to explore experiences of working with adult learners around the globe. They provide international mini case studies and show how different approaches were used to implement the same three-stage science education model. Rannikmäe, Holbrook and Cavas introduce a model that can be used as a tool for establishing the relevance of science education at all levels including lifelong learning. The authors of this chapter suggest that the challenge an adult educator faces in promoting decision-making in an international environment includes facets such as risk assessment, sustainable development, environmental issues, economic factors, political considerations, an entrepreneurial approach and ethical and moral aspects.

The final chapter by Fehring is a summary of how the chapters in this book demonstrate that adult learners bring with them a variety of learning backgrounds, a wealth of prior experiences and an array of different reasons for (re)engaging in learning as an adult. Some adult learners will be juggling family commitment, full-time employment and their learning commitments. Some may come with a catalogue of previous experience, which may also include failure in previous learning endeavours. Some bring cultural and language challenges while others may arrive with impairments. Their reasons for being coached, mentored, supervised or taught may vary from the quest for a formal qualification to further career opportunities, or may result from a non-voluntary institutional requirement for professional development programmes. As a result their learning needs, motivation levels and prior experience will vary. As mentors, coaches, tutors or supervisors we need to consider these diverse prior experiences, the array of incentives and the variety of learning needs when interacting with adult learners and when designing environments and materials for adult learners.

## Summary

The chapters that follow are not intended to mark the distinctions between those who mentor, coach, supervise or teach, which is why we have tended to use the term adult educator to represent mentor, coach, supervisor and teacher. For regardless of these labels, and their perceived and realised differences, adult educators will at some stage include an element of coaching, mentoring, supervising and teaching. Thus the balance of these facets within any given situation will vary.

The chapters that follow are intended to help you as an adult educator to reflect on your approach with a view to informing your professional practice and with a view to increasing adult learning efficiency. The book is intended to be of use to those involved in working with adult learners, rather than be a book about adult learners.

## References

Armstrong, C., Armstrong, D. and Spandagou, I. (2010). *Inclusive education: International policy and practice.* London: SAGE.

Beijaard, D., Meijer, P. C. and Verloop, N. (2004). Reconsidering research on teachers' professional identity. *Teaching and Teacher Education*, 20, 107–128.

Davis, K. S. (2001). 'Peripheral and subversive': Women making connections and challenging the boundaries of the science community. *Science Education*, 85, 368–409.

Hart, S., Dixon, A., Drummond, M. J. and McIntyre, D. (2004). *Learning without limits.* Maidenhead: Open University Press

McAlpine, L., Weston, C., Beauchamp, C., Wiseman, C. and Beauchamp, J. (1999). Building a metacognitive model of reflection. *Higher Education*, 37(2), 105–131.

Packard, B. W. (2003). Web-based mentoring: Challenging traditional models to increase women's access. *Mentoring & Tutoring*, 11(1), 53–65.

Schön, D. A. (1983). *The reflective practitioner: How professionals think in action.* London: Temple Smith.

Schön, D. A. (1987). *Educating the reflective practitioner: Toward a new design for teaching and learning in the professions.* San Francisco: Jossey-Bass.

Vygotsky, L. S. (1998). The problem of age (M. Hall, Trans.). In R. W. Rieber (ed.), *The collected works of L. S. Vygotsky: Vol. 5. Child psychology* (pp. 187–205). New York: Plenum Press.

Chapter 1

# Adult learning and the mentoring and coaching of teachers

*Rita Ellul and Heather Fehring*

## Introduction

This chapter discusses the main principles of adult learning as a context for effective professional learning that is tailored to the diverse cognitive and/or affective needs of adult learners in a variety of learning environments. Adult learning can be a challenging area for educators. For some adult educators, their role is clearly defined as a coach, a mentor or a supervisor. For others, their role may require a blend of these differing roles, depending not only on the course or programme, but also on the differing needs and status of the adult learners.

This chapter highlights some of the key features of the distinction between coaching and mentoring practices, and the essential professional development strategies needed when teaching adult learners in school settings. Developing appropriate learning opportunities, which address any content requirements, need to be underpinned by approaches which take into account both the professional and personal needs of the adult learners.

## Educational context

Education systems worldwide provide professional learning opportunities for a myriad of purposes encompassing policy change, new curriculum content knowledge, pedagogical strategies initiatives, development of new Information and Communication Technologies capabilities, and the list goes on. High-performing systems around the world focus on professional learning that improves classroom learning and teaching (Hattie, 2009; Jensen et al., March 2014). In the context of the Australian educational systems, the Australian Institute for Teaching and School Leadership (AITSL) is one system that is driving the agenda of change for professional learning initiatives. In a fluid and fast-changing environment, teachers must keep up with current teaching practices and policy changes in environments where they often have no voice in determining or influencing the timing of any ensuing changes or requirements.

With the many demands made of time-poor teachers, dedicating the time to undertake professional learning, time away from the classroom and completing any necessary pre-course or in-course learning tasks is challenging. For school leaders there are the added challenges of assessing where they will get best value for money that translates into improved student learning outcomes and a more highly skilled professional workforce. There is also the consideration of the different ways in which adults like to learn and what they value enough to dedicate the time and intellectual investment required in order to maximise the potential of the learning opportunity. Astute, strategic thinking is required by teachers and school leaders alike in order to identify professional learning that aligns best with adult learning principles and the identified needs of adult learners to make a positive impact on their learning.

Adult learning is a complex area. The learning needs of adults within their work, career and personal contexts, along with the life and work experiences they bring create the need for different approaches to the planning and delivery of professional learning opportunities to adults. The strategies and approaches used for the teaching of children do not necessarily apply to the teaching of adults. Malcolm Knowles' research into andragogy, which he defines as 'the art and science of helping adults learn' (1970), distinguishes adult learning from pedagogy, the art and science of teaching children. Andragogy addresses the different ways that adults learn and so differentiates it from childhood education.

Andragogy is a learner-centred approach and is based on six underlying assumptions, expanded from the original four developed in the 1970s, and these strengthen its differentiation from child-focused education. These assumptions inform an approach to learning in which the learner:

- needs to know the purpose of the learning before undertaking it;
- has an independent self-concept and can direct her/his own learning;
- brings life experiences from which to draw upon;
- is ready to learn;
- is a problem-based learner, wanting to apply her/his learning immediately to an issue at hand; and
- is internally motivated to learn (Knowles et al., 2015).

These assumptions can be used by instructors or facilitators to inform the way in which they structure professional learning to optimise meaningful engagement by the adult learners and impact on the practices of teachers and school leaders.

Knowles et al. (2015) present the andragogical model as a process model, which provides 'procedures and resources for helping learners acquire information and skills' (p. 51). The process commences with the facilitator establishing a positive climate for learning and enables a collaborative approach between facilitator and adult learner in which elements such as mutual planning, identifying the needs for learning, developing the programme objectives, designing the learning experiences, evaluating the learning outcomes and identifying new needs inform the next cycle. Andragogy provides a lens through which to re-assess the planning of professional learning in a way that understands and respects teachers as adult learners.

Professional learning is a vital component of any education system if it is to maintain a high standard of teaching and retain a high-quality teacher workforce (OECD, 2009). There is a vast range of professional learning opportunities available to teachers at any time, such as workshops, conferences, seminars, classroom walk-throughs, coaching and mentoring to name just a few; these can be delivered face-to-face, online or through a blended learning mix of the two. With such a range available, it would seem that adult learning would be a regular practice in the culture of schools (Stoll et al., 2006). However, the purpose of professional learning is to improve student learning; building teacher capacity is not an end in itself but a critical means with which to achieve this goal. Research shows that teachers are the most important variant on the level of student learning and achievement (Hattie, 2012). In this pre-eminent influencing role, it is essential that there is an ongoing approach to improving teacher skills. By the very nature of the students they teach, teachers' professional learning needs will vary as the needs, challenges, interests and habits of their students change, further strengthening the imperative for making ongoing professional learning.

The challenge for school leaders lies in understanding how to develop professional learning that is the most effective in building teacher capacity that will impact on student learning while meeting the needs of the adult learner. Effective professional learning, as with any meaningful learning, needs to take place over time, with opportunities to reflect, plan, learn with colleagues and receive feedback, with the learning taking place on site at the place where the actual work occurs (Ingvarson, 2003). Darling-Hammond and McLaughlin (1995) also identified professional learning as needing to be collaborative, sustained and intensive, involving problem-solving around specific problems of practice and supported by coaching. Characteristics such as these make the case for a move away from the 'one-hit' workshop or conference if long-term and sustained change in practice is to be achieved. Discrete isolated skill-based professional activities and out-of-context clinic-type professional sessions have long been discredited if sustained change to practice is required by adult learners in the workplace. Such learning is associated with notions of Work Integrated Learning (WIL) professional activities and the development of workplace partnerships where mentoring and coaching practices can be integrated in authentic practices.

Jensen et al.'s, (March, 2014) research into high-performing systems around the world identified intensive professional learning programmes with similar elements including teacher mentoring and coaching. From studies undertaken by OECD (2011) and Barber and Mourshed (2007) they concluded 'effective mentoring and coaching helps teachers diagnose their students' learning needs, and develop classroom management skills and pedagogy specific to their subjects' (Jensen et al., 2014, p. 7). Mentoring and coaching, if properly resourced, could be used to underpin the strategies identified by Darling-Hammond and McLaughlin (1995) and Jensen et al. (2014) to optimise their potential for achieving positive impact in the classroom. They also align with adult learning principles as the following section demonstrates.

## Mentoring and peer coaching strategies

The concepts of mentoring and coaching are not neatly differentiated in the literature. There are elements common to both strategies, such as the building and sustaining of trusting, confidential relationships and the appropriate matching of mentor–mentee or coach–coachee. Mentoring and coaching are also professional learning strategies, which can be used to support the development of teachers, regardless of content area or school context.

Mentor was a character in Homer's Odyssey, in which as a wise and faithful advisor, he was entrusted to protect the son of Odysseus while he went off to battle. A mentor is considered to have experience and wisdom that can be shared with a novice or someone less experienced, helping significant transitions in knowledge or work (Clutterbuck, 2014). Mentoring can involve additional behaviour such as counselling and professional friendship (Rhodes et al., 2004). It is a supportive process with mentor and mentee coming together to focus on the area of need identified by the mentee. This may vary from a novice mentee having a vague idea of what they need to know through to a mentee who may have some of the broader knowledge and experience but requires the more in-depth knowledge and understanding of an experienced colleague. In education, pre-service teachers and teacher graduates are commonly assigned a mentor to guide and advise them as they commence their professional journey. However, even more experienced teachers could find themselves at a 'novice' stage later in their career, for example through a transfer to a new school or progress to a new role.

Consider the following scenarios.

### Scenario 1

Olivia is completing a Master of Teaching Practice (Secondary). After a few days into her school placement, her supervising teacher asks her to plan and teach a differentiated mathematics lesson based on the current focus of algebra, which is to cater for the diverse needs of her Year 8 class. Olivia is confident with the content, but has no idea how to set up the class so that she can manage students working on different tasks. Olivia decides to seek her mentor's help in preparing for the lesson.

### Scenario 2

Mark has three years' teaching experience, all of which have been as a classroom teacher for senior primary students. In developing the school's workforce plan for the coming year, Mark's principal asks him if he would consider taking on the role of Physical Education (PE) teacher across the whole school as there will be vacancy in this position, knowing that it is an area in which Mark has a keen interest. Mark is excited by the prospect, but does not know what might be involved in planning and overseeing a whole school programme. He decides he will approach the mentor who had supported him in his first two years at the school and with whom he still maintains informal contact.

In these scenarios, both Olivia and Mark can seek the support and guidance of their mentors in areas where their knowledge and skills are limited. Their mentors in turn draw from their own experience and knowledge to help their mentees explicitly address these needs. Table 1.1 highlights some of the approaches that the mentors could use.

*Table 1.1* Possible mentoring approaches

*Olivia's mentor could:*

- Share and discuss sample plans which demonstrate differentiated learning, exploring the student outcomes to be addressed as well as the pedagogical strategies identified
- Highlight professional reading on differentiated learning that Olivia could draw upon as she plans her lesson
- Model a lesson for Olivia to observe and follow up with a discussion about what was observed
- Set up opportunities for Olivia to observe other classes where teachers use a range of strategies to plan and deliver lesson that cater for the needs of all students
- Develop the lesson plan collaboratively with Olivia
- Go through the lesson plan with Olivia before the lesson is given and provide feedback
- Work with Olivia to rehearse the way in which she will introduce the lesson and set up the learning tasks
- Team-teach part or all of the lesson with Olivia so that Olivia can observe how the lesson unfolds from a different perspective.

*Mark's mentor could:*

- Provide access for Mark to the curriculum planning, assessment, scheduling and other supporting documents for the current year's PE programme
- Arrange for the current PE teacher to meet with Mark to talk about the programme and respond to his questions (mentor could also attend)
- Arrange for Mark to work-shadow the PE teacher for one day, which will include a team-planning meeting; follow up with Mark after the work-shadowing to discuss his observations and perceptions about the role
- Arrange for Mark to meet with and observe two other PE teachers in neighbouring schools to look at other possible models of PE programmes
- Meet to debrief with Mark to check in on any of the discussions and observations he may have completed and identify any further questions he may have. At this meeting, mentor could also ask Mark about his possible career aspirations.

The mentors may suggest any number of these approaches to their mentees from which to select the most appropriate for their needs at the time. They may choose to progress through the suite of suggestions as a more comprehensive approach to their professional learning, modifying the tasks over time as their skills and understanding develops, while their mentors guide and support.

Coaching is about facilitating the learning process with the coachees. It is a process that helps them to learn, eliciting solutions from them and enabling learning and development to occur (Hoult, 2005). Hattie (2012) is explicit in differentiating mentoring and coaching, putting the focus of coaching specifically on student outcomes and writes coaching 'is not reflection; it is not self-awareness; it is not mentoring or working alongside. Coaching is deliberate actions to help the adults to get the results from the students – often by helping teachers to interpret evidence about the effect of their actions, and providing them with choices to more effectively gain these effects' (pp. 71–72).

Joyce and Showers (1982) were leaders in the use of coaching in schools, researching this area since the 1980s and they saw the coaching element as essential to support the transfer of skills and understanding into changed practice in the classroom.

Joyce and Showers use the term 'peer coaching', with a colleague as the coach and where both parties are equal, learning together and supporting each other. As the peer coach is a colleague, the process can 'contribute to the connection between peer coach and learner [coachee] as there is an understanding and first-hand experience of the environment in which the learning takes place' (Ellul, 2010, p. 16). A peer coach needs to create trusting relationships, critically listen and observe, ask skilful questions and guide reflective conversations (Boyd, 2006). With these elements in place, peer coaches are able to work collaboratively to improve an area of need identified by the coachee, and similarly to the role of mentee, with the coachee actively defining and directing his/her learning experience.

Consider these coaching scenarios.

## Scenario 3

Terry is an experienced teacher and has a Year 1 class, a year level she has not taught before. She and her peer coach Alexandra, a colleague who also has a Year 1 class, collaboratively plan units of work to identify the outcomes of the unit, assessments and some of the learning tasks. Both Terry and Alexandra take turns in coaching each other using a cycle of observation and feedback at least once a term, which is a model supported across the school.

In their pre-observation planning meeting, Terry highlights her concern about the lack of progress many of her students are making with spelling.

## Scenario 4

Adam is an experienced Maths and Science teacher and in the first year of a role as Head of the Science Faculty. Following a preliminary analysis of student data in science at the end of the first semester, he has led two sessions with the Science Faculty to discuss the data but his attempts to lead a deeper analysis with the team were met with little engagement. Adam would like to improve the situation so approaches his peer coach Rachel who is Head of the English Faculty.

The sample coaching questions in Table 1.2 demonstrate a range of clarifying and open-ended questions through which a coach could facilitate a conversation and where the coachee, in considering the questions in relation to her/his needs, would develop possible actions that would lead to the identification of a solution

*Table 1.2* Possible coaching approach

*Terry's Peer Coach Alexandra:*

- Why don't we start with a look at some writing samples from low, middle and high achieving students and compare results?
- Which students in particular are you concerned about and how does their data compare to the class average?
- Are there specific weaknesses, habits or approaches used by these students that you have been able to identify?
- There are a few spelling strategies that we both use in our classes? Can you give me a snapshot of other strategies you are currently using in your spelling programme?
- Which ones do you think are the most effective and how do you know?
- How could you monitor these strategies to gauge their effectiveness?
- When I come into your class next week what aspect/s of your spelling programme would you like me to focus on?

*Adam's Peer Coach Rachel:*

- I have had a similar experience myself. I found that by writing down my reflections about how the meetings I had with the team played out I was able to see some of the issues. For example, how did you structure the meetings, what questions did you ask the team and what discussion followed?
- What were the positives that resulted from these meetings?
- What challenges did these meetings present for you?
- Let's see if we can work out together what might be the possible reasons why the team hasn't come on board with a look at the data during the team meetings?
- First, why do you think looking at the data is important across the team?
- Secondly, what would a good data conversation sound and look like in your team?
- I found that demonstrating to my team how understanding the data helps improve their teaching practice improved the engagement of staff.
- How can you present the data in a different way that has more meaning and interest to the team?
- How might you support individual team members to better prepare to have a robust discussion about data without feeling threatened or anxious?

to his/her problem or progress towards an overall goal. The agency lies with the coachee, with the coach's role as one of opening up options and alternatives through collegiate questioning and interaction.

There is much more to mentoring and coaching than these scenarios suggest. Mentoring and coaching are longer term strategies; they need time for relationships to become established, strategies to be tried and tested, for learning to inform practice and ultimately for that practice to become embedded and impact on student learning. For the mentoring and coaching relationships to be effective, you as a mentor and coach must be 'professionally available', i.e. committed to investing time and skill to support the professional growth of the mentee or coachee. There needs to be a professional rapport between the partners that is based on trust and respect so that conversations can be open, confidentiality is maintained and no judgement made. Mentors and coaches also need to have the skills of active listening in order to engage deeply and understand the needs of the mentees or coachees and provide the level of support needed to help them to manage their own learning.

Mentees and coaches also have a role in supporting and maintaining a climate conducive to learning, by demonstrating a commitment to their learning and being open to dialogue. They need to be active learners, in completing the action(s) agreed upon, and also in reflecting on their practice, in sharing their reflection with their mentor and coach and in giving and receiving feedback.

Beyond the immediate mentor–mentee or coach–coachee relationships is a range of elements needed at the school level to support the effectiveness of these professional learning strategies. Embedding mentoring and/or coaching in the teaching and learning culture of the school requires commitment to the careful matching of mentoring and coaching pairs in order to optimise the potential for success; resourcing of the mechanisms through which the partnerships can be established and flourish, such as time for mentoring and coaching pairs to meet formally and procedures or guidelines which set out the expectations and responsibilities of all participants. Elements such as these are needed for the mentoring and coaching programmes to be developed and sustained and to be regarded as effective and valued professional learning strategies.

Depending on the needs of their colleagues, coaches in particular may find that they need to draw skilfully on their repertoire as both mentor and coach consciously adjusting their approach as the confidence, skills and understanding of their peer develops.

Adult learning principles are deeply embedded in the practices of mentoring and coaching. Mentees and coachees shape their own learning agenda with the support of their mentors and coaches. They understand the purpose of their learning as the responsibility for making the choices about what will be the focus of their learning and how they will learn. In understanding the value of the skills and understanding they are seeking to develop, mentees and coachees also demonstrate their motivation and their preparedness to learn.

Skilled mentors and coaches have a pivotal role in constructing the framework which will support their mentees and coachees to lead their own learning. In the strategies presented in the scenarios for Olivia and Mark, their mentors identified possible resources or concrete experiences which required them to be actively engaged, to explore, reject, trial, re-shape or seek further clarification in order to progress their professional growth. The importance of self-agency is of even greater importance in a coaching partnership, where coaching questions guide the coachee towards identifying the possible solution/s, in a partnership where they can test their ideas and check their understandings. The coaches, Alexandra and Rachel, in the scenarios described in Table 1.2 used their questioning techniques to support their coachees, Terry and Adam, to reflect on their current situations informed by evidence and from this identify possible actions they could take.

An understanding of adult learning principles can inform the structure of professional learning programmes to maximise their potential for the successful achievement of the programme outcomes and as we have seen, these principles align closely with mentoring and coaching. As professional learning strategies, mentoring and coaching focus directly on the needs of the learner, in a collaboration where mentees and coachees as learners actively identify their learning needs and direct their learning agenda with the support of their mentor or coach.

## Provocation

Choosing effective and efficient mentoring or peer coaching practices for adult learners requires professional educators to consider a range of options. The following ideas are considerations that will facilitate the selection of the needs of the adult learner and the nature of the professional development activity.

- Initially get to know the adult learners you will be working with and ascertain their background and previous experiences before designing the professional development structure and activities. This could be undertaken by an online survey.
- If you are planning a peer coaching programme, consider how you could structure opportunities for the peer coaches to work together in a collegiate, interactive and mutually supportive learning context at different stages to share and embed effective coaching practices.
- If you are introducing a programme, resource or strategy at the whole school, year or faculty levels, consider how this process could be facilitated by a mentoring approach where one member of the team is already experienced with the programme to be implemented so can act as an expert resource while providing collegial support to the team.

## References


AITSL (Australian Institute for Teaching and School Leadership). (2012). Australian Charter for the Professional Learning of Teachers and School Leaders. A shared responsibility and commitment August 2012. http://aitsl.edu.au/docs/default-source/default-documentlibrary/australian_charter_for_the_professional_learning_of_teachers_and_school_leaders.pdf?sfvrsn=4

Barber, M. and Mourshed, M. (September, 2007). How the world's best-performing schools come out on top. Retrieved 1 June 2015, from http://mckinseyonsociety.com/downloads/reports/Education/Worlds_School_Systems_final.pdf

Boyd, J. (2006). *Coaching in context.* Melbourne: Department of Education and Early Childhood Development. https://www.eduweb.vic.gov.au/edulibrary/public/teachlearn/student/coachingin context.pdf

Clutterbuck, D. (2014). *Everyone needs a mentor.* London: Chartered Institute of Personnel and Development.

Darling Hammond, L. and McLaughlin, M. W. (1995). Policies that support professional development in an era of reform. *Phi Delta Kappan,* 76(8), 597–604.

Ellul, R. (2010). ICT peer coaches: Techno-pedagogues of the twenty-first century. Unpublished PhD dissertation, School of Education, RMIT University, Melbourne, Victoria, Australia.

Hattie, J. (2009). *Visible learning: A synthesis of over 800 meta-analyses relating to achievement.* London: Routledge.

Hattie, J. (2012). *Visible learning for teachers. Maximizing impact on learning.* London: Routledge.

Hoult, G. (2005). Coaching educators: Fad, fashion or valuable new approach to developing and supporting our key people? (Occasional paper). Melbourne: Incorporated Association of Registered Teachers of Victoria.

Ingvarson, L. (2003). *Building a learning profession.* Retrieved 16 May 2015, from http://research.acer.edu.au/cgi/viewcontent.cgi?article=1004&context=professional_dev

Jensen, B., Hunter, J., Sonnemann, J. and Cooper, S. (March, 2014). Making time for great teaching. Grattan Institute Melbourne. Report No. 2014-3. Retrieved 16 May 2015 from http://grattan.edu.au/wp-content/uploads/2014/03/808-making-time-for-great-teaching.pdf

Joyce, B. and Showers, B. (1982). The coaching of teaching. *Educational Leadership,* 40(1), 4–10.

Knowles, M. S. (1970). *The modern practice of adult education: Andragogy versus pedagogy.* New York: The Association Press.

Knowles, M. S., Holton, E. F. and Swanson, R. A. (2015). *The adult learning: The definitive classic in adult education and human resource development.* 8th edn. London: Routledge.

OECD. (2009). Creating effective teaching and learning environments: First results from TALIS. Retrieved 14 June 2015, from www.oecd.org/edu/school/43023606.pdf

OECD. (2011). Lessons from PISA for the United States. Strong performers and successful reformers in education. Retrieved 1 June 2015, from http://www.oecd.org/education/school/43023606.pdf

Rhodes, C., Stokes, M. and Hampton, G. (2004). *A practical guide to mentoring, coaching and peer-networking: Teacher professional development in schools and colleges.* London: Routledge Falmer.

Stoll, L., Bolam, R., McMahon, A., Wallace, M. and Thomas, S. (2006). Professional learning communities: A review of the literature. *Journal of Educational Change*, 7(4), 221–258.

Chapter 2

# Professional identity

## Insights, strategies and approaches

*Carey Normand and Maureen Morriss*

Professional identity is one of those things that despite your attention to it, or not, you will be creating one. It is in our own interests, as professionals, to establish our credibility as lecturers/teachers/educators. It is imperative to consider what and how our professional identity forms and how it can be enhanced so that what we want others to see/believe about us aligns with our own perceptions of what we want. In this chapter we will explore the concept of professional identity through a close investigation and critique of the literature on professional identity and, to an extent, on professionalism (for more information on professionalism and professional development see Chapter 4 in this book). We will also examine strategies, approaches and techniques that may help you as an adult educator in support of the formation of professional identity.

### Professionalism

It is widely recognised that there is no single definition of professionalism and other related notions, for example, professionality, profession, professional identity and professionalisation (Erde, 2008). Professionalism can be seen as a concept or idea that '... points in many different directions' (Gewirtz et al., 2009, p. 3). Gerwirtz et al. (2009, p. 3) think that two directions are worth signalling: the first 'points in the direction of "profession"' as 'a category of occupational classification'; and the second points in the direction of 'professional virtues' described by Gewirtz et al. (2009) as 'categorizations of technical and ethical standards claimed on behalf of certain occupational roles' (p. 3). This conceptualisation is useful as it succinctly relates occupational roles with concomitant characteristic standards and codes of (ethical) behaviour. It can also be seen as problematic in that it signals 'the exclusionary nature of professions' and 'their claims to special status and influence over others' (Gewirtz et al. 2009, p. 3). Gewirtz et al. (2009) argue that to understand teacher professionalism it is critical to 'work with plural conceptions of professionalism' (p. 3) and to do this 'dialectically' (p. 4). Consequently, it is important to identify adult educators' professionalism by analysing their occupational role(s), the standards and codes of practice adhered to and of power relations legitimised by belonging to an 'exclusionary' body.

Increasingly, it is argued within the literature, that personal identity constructs and collective or organisational constructs of identities are misaligned and incongruous. Evetts (2009) argued that 'we seem to be witnessing the development of two different (and in many ways contrasting) forms of professionalism in knowledge-based, service-sector work: organizational and occupational professionalism' (p. 23). 'Organizational professionalism' (p. 23) is what she calls the 'discourse of control' (p. 23) is used by the employers and managers and is a form of managerialism i.e. it is based on bureaucratic and hierarchical structures, target setting, performance management, regulation and increased standardisation. 'Occupational professionalism' (p. 23) is markedly different and is exemplified by 'discourse constructed within professional occupational groups' (p. 23) and conforms to more classical definitions of professionalism which are about collegiality, autonomy, self-regulation, control over one's own work, discretion and professional ethics and codes of behaviour 'monitored by institutions and associations' (Evetts, 2009, p. 23). As an adult educator you may want to consider what essentially, Evetts' (2009) research highlights as the tension between the two competing types of professionalism with their very different behavioural codes. Furthermore, there is a shift in power, control and agency from the individual professional, as a member of a professional occupational group, to that which is located within a managerial group, who standardise work practices within a marketised, privatised and consumer-orientated policy context. Having awareness of this tension is important to adult educators as there will be times when you as an adult educator feel that your own values, beliefs and practices are being challenged or undermined. It is, therefore, important to have a clear sense of your professional identity and this develops through an understanding of occupational norms as practised by the occupational group. Later in the chapter, we will explore some of these occupational practices for educators.

Critical, then, to this discussion on professionalism is the relationship between the individual professional adult educator and the organisation, the wider political, social and cultural environment and the policy context. The tension lies in the ways in which professional adult educators see themselves as individuals and as a collective and the ways in which their employers, society and the policy makers also see them, and allow them to be seen.

## Professional identity

### *Insights*

In a literature review on professional identity, undertaken by Beijaard et al. (2004), the authors found that there was no clear definition of professional identity but that the research literature on teachers' professional identity could be divided into three categories, namely: (1) identity formation; (2) identification of the characteristics; and (3) teachers' representations in their stories or narrative accounts. From this review, Beijaard et al. (2004), concluded that there were 'four essential features of teachers' professional identity': first, that it was an '*ongoing process*' that was dynamic and 'not stable or fixed'; secondly, that it constituted both the '*person and context*' and, therefore, illustrated that teachers will behave differently in different contexts based on their own value base and their 'own teaching culture'; thirdly, that 'a teacher's professional identity consists of *sub-identities*', again linked to the person, experience and to her/his relationships within a context; and fourthly, that teachers are active engagers in the process of 'professional identity formation' and it is not so much about what they have but about how they use this '... to make sense of themselves as teachers' i.e. have '*agency*' (Beijaard et al., 2004, p. 122–123; emphasis in original). These findings are interesting as they show that professional identity is not a thing, a list of characteristics or a set of behaviours and codes but, rather, it is a way of being that is contingent upon personal, social and cultural constructs. This distinction is important as it links to a particular view of identity that is developmental, socially and culturally mediated and is related to your conception of 'self'. Professional identity then is felt by adult educators and embedded in their behaviours. Consequently, equilibrium relies on the synergy or alignment between the adult educators' professional identity and that of the institutional environment in which they work. Beijaard et al. (2004) noted that sub-identities should be harmonised as these are at the core of professional identity and if the professional experiences conflict, for example, 'educational change or change in their immediate working environment' (p. 122) it will be very hard for them to make the change. This is often interpreted by employers, managers and policy makers as resistance to change or stubbornness but Beijaard, et al. (2004) argue that 'the more central a sub-identity is, the more costly it is to change or lose that identity' (p. 122) (which, as said earlier, is a fundamental state of being).

As an adult educator you will have to consider the key theme identified in the point above: the relationship between standardised behaviours – uniformity and conformity – and professional identity. In recent years there has been a move towards standardising behaviours and measuring these through competency audits. This conflicts with Beijaard et al's. (2004) findings that teachers' actively engage in a (lifelong) process of professional identity formation and through this find their 'authentic and discursive self' (p. 112). This self, drawing on Dillabough's (1999) work, 'arises out of complex and meaningful social interactions with peers and other "professionals"' (Beijaard et al., 2004, p. 114) and not out of an instrumental and competency dominated teaching environment.

Many of the studies analysed in the Beijaard, et al. (2004) literature review, referred to 'lay theories' (p. 114), which are personally constructed by the adult educator and are otherwise referred to as 'tacitly acquired understandings' (p. 114) or personal theories. As an adult educator your personal experiences, including childhood, and early teaching role models, all contribute to lay theories about professional identity. In a study of Further Education (FE) lecturers' professional identity formation, Bathmaker and Avis (2007) found that preconceived, or idealised notions of lecturer identity, not only influenced trainees' expectations about 'how they should behave' but also led to tensions as they struggled with these idealised concepts and the contradictory reality they experienced in the role.

A literature review by Trede et al. (2012) on the development of professional identities led the authors to conclude that there is a 'vast body of literature on professional identity which does not seem to be integrated by higher education research' (p. 382) and, overall, there is 'underdevelopment of the research base for professional identity development formation' (p. 379).

These findings are pertinent to this chapter as they provide some insight and understanding of teachers, educators and coaches' professional identity. What is clear is that it is not one identity but rather a multiplicity of identities that reflect the personal contexts. Professional identity is socially situated within occupational groups and understood relationally i.e. between individuals and groups and organisations. This point is important as often we think of teaching as fitting neatly into a pre-defined box; however, the reality is that teaching can be many things, for example, facilitation, instruction, modelling, didactic, dialogical, and adult educators are arguably more heterogeneous than homogenous as an occupational group. One reason for this is that they have different subject disciplines and much of their professional identity comes from this source, that is, they identify with being a historian, dentist or biologist. As an adult educator it is worth reflecting on where your professional identity originates and, further, to consider the relationship that exists between your subject discipline knowledge, behaviours and identity and your 'teaching' knowledge, behaviours and identity. Another reason for this is that organisations have a culture. The culture of an organisation is determined by its mission, purpose and structures but more so by the people that work in it. Increasingly in educational and service organisations there has been a growth in administrators and managers and this has led to a change in the organisational culture, shifting from, for example, a focus on learning to creating standards for teaching and learning, by administrators. The adult educator's professional identity is being influenced by her/his internal constructs and as a response to these many external constructs. In many senses becoming a professional is successfully navigating through the personal, occupational and organisational landscapes.

Critical to any professional identity is the fundamental principle of autonomy and, through this, agency, that is, the adult educator's ability to make her/his own professional judgements and control her/his own behaviour and professional practices. From the literature, it is evident that for many this aspect of professional identity has been diminished or eroded and the perception is of not being 'allowed' autonomy at a structural level. This has resulted in the paradoxical position of the ***managed professional*** lecturer. Further, it individualises adult educators and their practices and frames them within a narrow field, which is essentially between the individual and their manager. This form of micromanagement fails to recognise the multiplicities of professional identities and negates the collegiality and the formation of communities of practice. As a consequence, the strategies and techniques to facilitate the formation of professional identity will necessarily be multifarious and context orientated, if not specific.

## Strategies and approaches to support your 'professional identity'

The purpose of this section of our chapter is to highlight some of the strategies and approaches that you as an adult educator can use to assist the development of professional identity. It is by no means an exhaustive set but it does highlight some of the key elements that all professionals consider, whether consciously or subconsciously.

As seasoned adult educators we have had many experiences that have enabled us to consider how to foster and support professional identity within the teaching and learning context. The following discussion relates to some of the practical elements that may occur when assisting another or considering your own professional identity formation, development and enhancement.

The two main contexts that we will use to provide examples of the ways in which professional identity can be fostered are; first, as lecturers in the tertiary setting working with undergraduates and graduate students while they study in the field of primary/elementary/further education teaching. The second context is as independent consultants to elementary and middle schools, further and higher education settings. Both contexts assume a relationship between a novice and a more experienced practitioner. Of course, individuals can explore the strategies independently and thus continue to develop their own professional identity.

As outlined previously by Beijaard et al. (2004) there are four overarching elements that influence you as your professional identity develops. Fundamentally, this is not a stagnant process but rather one that is constantly in a state of change and is therefore an ongoing process: a continuum. This process is both conscious and subconscious and just as what motivates you is not fixed, similarly, your professional identity is fluid and developing: it is a state of being. It is within this element of change the other three elements of personal context, sub-identities and active engagement develop, thus developing your professional identity as a lifelong process. Consequently, you will be establishing your professional identity whether or not you explicitly set out to do so.

### *Strategies*

i) Professional engagement and learning – what motivates you at any given time directly affects your engagement in your work. Both your values and your circumstances contribute to your motivations. While this changes over time you need to understand and recognise what is most important to you and prioritise these elements.

In teaching we have found that beginning teachers often have a desire to assist students to be happy and content at school/college. This desire quickly changes to being able to assess skills and apply suitable strategies for their students to learn. Thus these beginning teachers activate their professional engagement as they meet the work situation and its demands.

ii) Enthusiasm is infectious – being upbeat about what you are interested in and engaged with people and the environment allows for others to perceive you as someone who is connected and enjoys the workplace interaction. Easy and genuine ways to project a positive attitude has an affect on others' perception of your professional identity.

Learning about professional practices is a major way to develop experience and gain an understanding about what are the 'best' practices in your field. Interacting with others with varying degrees of adult education experience allows you to consider the positive/negative elements and to decide what is most comfortable or right for you in your practices. As well as interactions in the moment, or during the teaching situation with others, learning can occur online through visual, audio and written text-based options. There are usually journals and magazines that you can subscribe to for particular types of information depending on your purpose. Participating in professional development seminars and workshops also enable learning to occur with a focus that is predetermined. Your reflective practices and subsequent actions that occur around your many and varied interactions as you learn will influence your professional identity and allow it to continue to evolve, remain open ended and forever be in a state of change.

### *Professional relationships and collaborations*

Fostering positive interactions with colleagues around work is an important part of developing professional relationships, networks and collaborations. It seems simple but a genuine friendly smile, some small talk, and interest in others does go a long way as you establish working relationships. It is necessary to intersperse the work orientated interactions with some more social ones as you collaborate together whether as partners or in teams. When your colleagues know a little about you personally it does make the working situation more positive.

The relationships you establish throughout your working life are not one sided and neither are they only in the workplace. While you should establish work-based relationships that foster and support your needs, they also need to be reciprocal. Something we have learned is that it is wise to use your skills to benefit the workplace first. Share your resources or ideas willingly. Let your colleagues and supervisors see your attributes and contributions – while you may have to do some on a voluntary basis you will reap the benefits in the long run. Adult education is a collaborative profession most of the time and it is in working and offering your talents and contributions to those that you work with directly that will enable you to receive in return. Thus sharing resources, ideas, asking questions, commenting and observing around the field that you are directly involved in contributes to your professional identity immediately and long term.

Showing that you are willing to do the 'grunt work', even though you may not prefer this, shares responsibilities and thus you can be seen as someone who is willing to step outside boundaries for the cause, in this case teaching. Volunteering for the more visible projects that may be more challenging for you also provides a view of your professionalism and dedication while growing your knowledge and understanding.

Being a 'team player' versus 'egocentrism' is an important distinction to remember when working with adult learners. The strength of character to admit mistakes, and take responsibility for those mistakes even when you feel embarrassed, will show others that you have integrity and are willing to be part of the collaborations in honest ways. Important too, in professional behaviours, is in taking calculated risks knowing that not all choices work out but at least you will show that you can take the initiative.

Building networks that will support and extend you in your field are also an effective support for you throughout your professional career. While these networks will mostly grow and change as you develop and change in your professional identity they are invaluable.

Some of these come in the form of the colleagues in your workplace but they can also be professional organisations that support your field. For example:

- alumni associations allow you to look beyond your profession and interact with people's thoughts and ideas in a wider circle;
- certification agencies (whether this is higher education, local professional development providers, and state or government bodies) can provide a platform for you to learn and engage with targeted opportunities to learn more in an ever-changing field of practice;
- joining a professional organisation that has as its aim the development in a particular field are ways to widen your network of professionals interested in the same or alternative areas that you are interested in. These organisations offer opportunities to interact with others, consider developing trends in research, discuss many of the practicalities of classroom responsibilities, and explore leadership within the field. They do this in a multitude of ways not only at conferences but also through text-based support, online resources, webinars, and other electronic means.

It is worthwhile remembering, as you forge new, or continue with established networks, to look for those that inspire or interest you and that you also feel you can call on or reach out to if necessary. Try to maintain links to the people, practices and developments that you feel engaged with and provide collaborative support.

## *Professional presence*

How is your presence perceived, by whom and in what instances? It is imperative to reflect upon the ways in which you interact when in formal and informal situations with peers, supervisors and colleagues when in professional settings. You need to participate where appropriate and take the lead if it is an area that is your responsibility. Be ready and prepared for anything – team meetings, classroom lessons, specialised events – preparing for your part and being responsible for all that entails as well as being flexible to meet any unexpected situations that are not within your immediate responsibility area.

Who you sit next to, can see or hear, line of vision of speaker or person holding the meeting or session influences your engagement with the subject. It also provides others with an insight into your professionalism. Your actions and ways of being are constantly under scrutiny by all around you. If you are holding the meeting or session – have the room organised so you can interact with all even if it is just by sight as this demonstrates you want to engage everyone.

*In meetings* you need to think about having a balance between speaking and listening. It is important to make thoughtful concise contributions and to tie in what you say to what others have said. Do not be the one who never participates. Thus think before you speak but know you do have valuable contributions to make.

*Body language* will also help you communicate effectively, provided it does not signal the opposite to what you intended. Frowning, tapping, staring into space and not showing your interest or engagement in the situation will have a negative affect on how you are perceived.

*Being on time* is also a factor that suggests how you value what it is you are attending. Despite what you may think, those making judgements will also look at your appearance, so dress appropriately – adjust your clothes to fit the occasion.

*How you express yourself* or your demeanour and the ways you interact on a day-to-day basis are also evidence of who you are and what identity you are portraying. Responding in a timely manner to requests, emails, texts, etc., sets up an idea about your efficiency and ability to be prompt. Thus this affects how you may appear to those you are interacting with and supporting. Listening carefully to others, thinking about another's perspective, withholding judgement until you have considered the person's point of view are all strategies that add to your professional image and identity.

*Online identity*, or your presence within social media, is a powerful tool to make connections with others, extend your learning and ask questions. But be aware that prospective employers and colleagues may search online for information about you and your identity. It is imperative that you consider your identity that is made public in this way – is it what you want everyone to know/see about you? Build your profile on a professional networking site such as 'LinkedIn' or post your own professional portfolio that you can share with those that you want to see some aspects of your professional identity. It is useful to remember that it is no longer a local identity but an international one. Emails, text messages, social media responses can be very public so you want to present who you are professionally. This may mean not giving too much detail or description and being succinct and not gossipy.

## Approaches

It is important to remind ourselves that we are in control of our own representation to others, to potential, employers, colleagues, reviewers, relatives, friends and so on. Highlighting your specific skills, your professional accomplishments/history, your experiences in your field, and your professional associations all contribute to your professional identity and contribute to the perception of you by others. So it is mindful of us to consider the purposes for which approach or combination of approaches we may use to build our professional identity. Is it related to job acquisition, job promotion, and presence in the field or perhaps for documentation, to name a few?

### *Professional portfolio*

An online portfolio can serve as an easy way to share elements pertaining to your professional identity. It is space for storage of documents that when viewed provide information about you professionally. Your résumé/curriculum vitae, experiences, projects, career highlights, areas of professional interest, attestations etc. can all become part of the picture you paint about yourself professionally. It is a simple way to share information on multiple platforms and an easy way to locate documents when you need them quickly (of course you can also have a hard copy of your documents). Linking your portfolio to other professional websites also allows your professional identity to be available.

There are many resources online to assist you with portfolio development and it is easy for a novice online user to develop. An important thing to remember about your professional portfolio is that you need to keep it up to date. It is not just a copy of your résumé, consider carefully what you want available for all to view, and do not include personal information, or personal contact details. Name and email should suffice if someone wants to contact you and then you can proceed further once you have verified the legitimacy of the person making contact.

### *Competence standards/frameworks and uniformity and conformity*

People you interact with are constantly making judgements about you and your professional identity whether you realise it or not. They have notions about your commitment, character, knowledge and competence. In most professional fields frameworks around the competences regarded as instrumental to that field are available. Recently there has been widespread discussion and mandates for monitoring teacher competence around the Danielson Framework (https://danielsongroup.org/framework/). The mandate mentioned is for the evaluation of teachers in the New York Public School System. There are four domains that this framework presents which are: planning and preparation; classroom environment; instruction; and professional responsibilities. It is interesting to reflect upon this and other frameworks and the elements that go into the ability to be a teacher. These elements all contribute to a teacher's professional identity. The way they are used in this instance is a subject for heated discussion but leaving that aside the framework allows teachers to know about expectations and they can use it as a measurement tool for their own personal development.

### *Decision making*

We are always making professional and personal decisions and we need to think about whether we are the type who make quick decisions, an 'on the spot' decision maker – or someone who considers and considers and considers – and never really makes a decision – 'a procrastinator'. The type of decision maker you are will affect positively or negatively your professional identity. Realising what circumstance needs more thought and should not be a snap decision or gut reaction will enable you to have a variety of strategies for making decisions. We recommend not making decisions in only one way but using a variety of ways. As an adult educator, establish an approach to decision making that can be flexible according to the situation or the decision making styles of others you work with.

To conclude, the importance of professional identity is situated in the ways in which adult educators act, interact and express themselves. The research clearly identifies the ways in which one's professional identity is formed and developed and the critical relationship between the person and the context. The practical section of this chapter articulates the ways in which educators can consider elements that are pertinent to developing and sustaining their professional identity in positive ways and, through active engagement, develop agency. We hope that as you begin, continue and come to the end of your career, you ruminate on the ways in which you can represent all that you are, hope you are, and what others think you are, in your element of the profession.

## Provocation

Reflect on your answer to the following question as this will help you to determine what, at this moment in time, your priorities are in relation to your professional identity.

> *What do I want my colleagues and my professional contemporaries to say about me when I am not in their presence?*

## References

Bathmaker, A.-M. and Avis, J. (2007). 'How do I cope with that?' The challenge of 'schooling' cultures in further education for trainee FE lecturers. *British Educational Research Journal*, 33 (4), 509–532.

Beijaard, D., Meijer, P. C. and Verloop, N. (2004). Reconsidering research on teachers' professional identity. *Teaching and Teacher Education*, 20, 107–128.

Danielson, C. (2013). The framework. https://danielsongroup.org/framework

Dillabough, J. A. (1999). Gender politics and conceptions of the modern teacher: Women, identity and professionalism. *British Journal of Sociology of Education*, 20 (3), 373–394.

Erde, E. L. (2008). Professionalism's facets: Ambiguity, ambivalence and nostalgia. *Journal of Medicine and Philosophy*, 33 (1), 6–26.

Evetts, J. (2009). The management of professionalism. In S. Gewirtz, P. Mahony, I. Hextall and A. Cribb (eds), *Changing teacher professionalism: International trends, challenges and ways forward* (pp. 19–30). London: Routledge.

Gewirtz, S., Mahony, P., Hextall, I. and Cribb, A. (2009). Policy, professionalism and practice: Understanding and enhancing teachers' work. In S. Gewirtz, P. Mahony, I. Hextall and A. Cribb (eds.), *Changing teacher professionalism: International trends, challenges and ways forward* (pp. 3–16). London: Routledge.

Higher Education Academy. (2011) The UK Professional Standards Framework for teaching and supporting learning in higher education. https://www.heacademy.ac.uk/sites/default/files/downloads/ukpsf_2011_english.pdf

Trede, F., Macklin, R. and Bridges, D. (2012). Professional identity development: A review of the higher education literature. *Studies in Higher Education*, 37 (3), 365–384.

Chapter 3

# Enhancing reflective practices in professional adult education

*Carolina Guzmán-Valenzuela and Valeria M. Cabello*

## Introduction

This chapter critically examines the concept of reflective practices in professional adult education. Reflective practices promote a situated construction of knowledge by questioning professionals' own taken-for-granted frames of reference and the creation of new interpretations of practices in specific contexts and in interaction with other colleagues. This way, reflective practices help to create new solutions for professional challenges.

In this chapter, we offer an overview of Schön's (1983, 1987) ideas about reflective practices in diverse professional settings and go beyond these ideas by stressing the importance of enhancing professional reflection systematically through collaborative ways. We also discuss the dynamic nature of professional knowledge as an amalgam of disciplinary frameworks and practical abilities that are in permanent development and interaction in particular professional environments. Finally, we propose some specific ways to enhance reflective practices in professional learning settings including some recommendations for action for mentors, supervisors, coaches and teachers of adult learners.

This chapter is addressed to professionals of diverse fields as reflective coaches, mentors and educators who are involved in any kind of post-secondary education, either in formal or non-formal settings, who are of course themselves professionals.

## Schön's epistemology of practice and his legacy

Donald Schön's legacy in education, especially in adult education, is undeniable. His books *The reflective practitioner: How professionals think in action* (1983) and *Educating the reflective practitioner: Toward a new design for teaching and learning in the professions* (1987) have helped the process of critically examining professional knowledge and the ways it is reached and developed. One of the most influential of his ideas is that professional knowledge is conceived not as a static object acquired by a learner but as a process in permanent movement and flux, and highly dependent on particular contexts that are also dynamic. From this perspective, professional knowledge involves not only a set of disciplinary frameworks, practical competencies and experience but also the capacity to solve singular problems that arise from particular situations and that pose dilemmas to professionals.

According to Schön (1983, 1987), professionals act in their daily practices in a spontaneous way by bringing into play a knowledge that has been generated from past experiences. This experiential knowledge is termed 'knowledge in action', rooted in practices, a knowledge that does not simply follow rules, procedures or instantiate formal knowledge. To a large degree, professional practical knowledge is tacit, so much so that professionals have difficulties in describing it (Polanyi, 1966). Nevertheless, new understandings can emerge when professionals encounter unexpected situations or when an intended practical solution does not work.

As an adult educator, an understanding of the concepts of 'reflection in action' and 'reflection on action' might help you. In the first case – reflection in action – a professional, while dealing with a new problem, tries to find possible explanations and, from these tentative hypotheses, tries to solve it. These possible explanations originate in a professional's knowledge in action already developed in the past when s/he solved similar previous problems. However, when a solution does not work, professionals might have to produce a new hypothesis about the problem situation and test them by following new courses of action. These new hypotheses about the problem might be produced and tested when the professional is *in* action (when the problem arises, perhaps unexpectedly) or *on* the action. In the first case, Schön talks about 'reflection in action' that enables the practitioner to connect with her/his prior knowledge and extant emotions to attend to a particular situation. In the second case, Schön refers to 'reflection on action'. Reflection on action is a retrospective action (McAlpine, Weston, Beauchamp, Wiseman and Beauchamp, 1999) that gives space and time to you as a professional to re-construct your professional actions, and re-analyse the explanations generated around a problem and the strategies used in order to solve it. Reflection in action helps professionals to change their courses of action in situ, whereas reflection on action has an impact on future actions.

Schön's theories have been useful in understanding professional knowledge as more than disciplinary knowledge. When experienced professionals deal with unexpected problems, they do not start from theoretical knowledge, which they then apply in addressing practical problems. They start with a reservoir of practical experience. However, problems are never identical and pose challenges, each having its particular sets of characteristics so calling for professional deliberation and carefully chosen action. Professionals use, therefore, an amalgam of knowledge drawn from both disciplinary frameworks acquired by formal education and from their own professional experience, which *together* help to provide resources for new explanations and solutions.

Schön's ideas have had an impact on the conception of educators themselves as professionals. His ideas challenged the conception of educators as mere executors of abilities and trained by others to solve generic educative problems. Their professional actions do not consist of aprioristic principles used to solve problems. Rather, professional action consists of a mix including propositional knowledge, process knowledge, practical knowledge, intentions, feedback (particularly self-monitoring) and having reasons against which they can be held accountable (Eraut, 1999).

Since Schön developed his ideas, there have been essentially two lines of critical comment and developments relevant here. The first is that of professionals being understood to act as part of professions as communities, an insight that has given rise to the concept of 'community of practice' (Wenger, 1999). The second is that Schön underplayed the significance of systematic knowledge. If we put a valuing of systematic knowledge together with informed and reasoned action, we are taken to the idea of the research base for professions being itself systematically developed. In turn, the desirability emerges of professionals themselves being involved in and being significant contributors in this research endeavor (see the Gibson, Holme and Taylor chapter in this book). As active and reflective professionals, teachers are well able to systematically research their practices, both within the teaching profession and in collaboration with university researchers.

## The nature of professional knowledge

In this section, we offer three remarks about the nature of professional knowledge. First, professional knowledge is composed not only of both disciplinary frameworks and practical abilities acquired during undergraduate formation but also it involves developmental knowledge. Professional knowledge acquired in a higher education programme (in both undergraduate, postgraduate and post-experience programmes through lifelong-learning) is a good starting point for professional performance. However, once it is brought into a professional context, it needs to be developed and expanded. Professional knowledge that is acquired through a formal process, then, is not sufficient to become a good professional (in terms of a professional who adequately meets professional challenges).

The development of professional knowledge is crucial since professional situations are changing, complex and they open spaces of uncertainty (if act (a), then what might follow?); old formulas do not always provide the foundations for solving new problems. It follows, too that your professional knowledge is not an endpoint with a permanent state but is continuous knowledge in progress; it needs to be developed and extended through professional practices. The concept of 'practical wisdom' (Phelps, 1991) offers the formation of a more sophisticated knowledge that has been extended and improved through situated practices. It is knowledge in movement, and can be thought of in terms of informal theories that practitioners develop from their own practical experience (Fook and Gardner, 2007).

Secondly, the relationship between theory and practice in the construction of professional knowledge is circular rather than linear. While acquiring disciplinary knowledge is basic when starting a professional life, practical knowledge embedded in practices situated in particular professional contexts helps to adapt, modify and create new knowledge when a professional dilemma appears and when a solution can be found neither in disciplinary knowledge nor in prior similar situations. But, in turn, the emergence of new situations (new diseases, new demographic patterns, new technologies) can prompt a search for relevant formal disciplinary knowledge, some of which itself might need to be developed.

Both kinds of knowledge (disciplinary and practical) and their constant interaction in particular professional contexts help professionals to create new interpretations around a problematic situation as well as to originate new and creative solutions. It follows, therefore, that your disciplinary knowledge and practical knowledge offer the professional resources through which you as an adult educator can address the situations that you encounter, and some of those situations might be novel. Sometimes, situations are unexpected so your prior knowledge resources might be inadequate. In those situations, you might find that your capabilities are inadequate and you might search for and assimilate relevant formal propositional knowledge and/or try to acquire systematically relevant new skills and/or new understandings in order to address your professional challenges. So arises the particular idea of professional creativity, namely the expansion by professionals of new practical principles, techniques, understandings-in-practice, and conceptions of presenting situations. All this in turn calls for virtuous circles of practice feedback, observation, systematisation and quality evaluations (through peer-analysis, benchmarking and so forth).

Thirdly, professional knowledge is dynamic. It might adapt, change and progress depending on particular settings in specific contexts or institutions. Institutions (of different kinds) have a particular ethos characterised by their own organisational cultures and social relationships. Out of an institutional ethos constructed meanings emerge, which give sense to institutional life. These meanings have been constructed through historical processes and are part of traditions, rules and ways of doing things within a culture or institution. Institutions, it might be said, have their own dominant 'imaginaries' (Taylor, 2007). In this sense, your professional knowledge is a situated knowledge in which your context helps to shape it and give sense to it.

However, characteristically, a complex institution or profession will exhibit diverse and even rivalrous views on matters. It follows that there are neither standard problems that can be solved through standardised ways nor unique solutions. Rather, a plethora of solutions might contribute to solve a particular problem in a successful way (or not). Further, there can be radically different – and maybe antagonistic – views as to what is to count as a success.

Reading, interpretations and possible solutions for educative problems might be offered by either individuals or a group. Depending on the culture of your institution, you as an adult educator might interpret and propose solutions to problems acting individually or as part of a professional community. In this latter case, both interpretations and possible solutions to problems are collectively constructed. Here, the concept of 'community of practice' (Wenger, 1999; Lave and Wenger, 1991) comes into play. A community of practice is composed of a group of people – say, members of an educational community – who share similar concerns, work on similar problems, engage in the pursuit of common goals, and, at the same time, learn from each other and act together to reach shared objectives (Wenger, 1999). Communities of practices are nurturing spaces for sharing reflections and constructing new meanings with others through critical reflection. A community of practice also provides opportunities for analysing settings, giving and receiving feedback about practices as well as suggestions for improving practices or solving problems professionally in varied contexts (Cabello and Topping, 2014).

## Enhancing reflective practices in professional learning settings

In this section, we refer to reflective practices in relation to educators in formal and non-formal settings of professional education, both initial professional education and post-experience education. The ideas of 'reflective teaching practices', 'reflection in action' and 'reflection on action' have become fuzzy concepts that are far from easy to capture or put into practice. In solving unexpected problems or addressing challenging situations, both reflection in action and reflection on action might help to create *new* solutions. However, it is important that difficulties and challenges as well as goals are clearly defined in order to generate adequate courses of action that address these situations. Adult educators as practitioners will be able to monitor whether they are solving a detected problem or addressing a complex situation and achieving their goals (McAlpine et al., 1999). In this sense, when you as an adult educator teach, you might try to develop a self-monitoring capacity, so that you are increasingly conscious of your own actions, are capable of detecting when a problem or a challenge arises and make explicit – at least to yourself – your implicit knowledge in order to redirect your actions to new possible solutions or courses of action.

Guzmán-Valenzuela and Barnett (2013), in analysing teaching difficulties among new lecturers, have shown that reflective practices are not always possible, especially in the case of inexperienced teachers. For them, the key issue about reflective practices has to do not with the reflective process itself but with the conceptualisation of a problem in the classroom by a teacher. In other words, the level of awareness adult educators have around certain difficulties they are experiencing when they teach is crucial here. In their study, Guzmán-Valenzuela and Barnett (2013) show that novice teachers might not always be able to visualise a problem (that can be detected by students or by an external observer). Problems may simply go unnoticed.

While expert teachers use intuitive and tacit knowledge to detect and deal with difficulties in the classroom and master a ***know-how*** (Knight, 2006) that allows them to read classroom events in a holistic way, novice teachers might tend to ignore difficult situations (Hogan, Rabinowitz and Craven, 2003) or not 'to read clues from teaching situations and the students' learning needs as they emerge in situ' (Guzmán-Valenzuela and Barnett, 2013, pp. 12-13). New teachers continue to focus on other kinds of teaching priorities in simply, as it were, coping with the pressure of the tasks. However, because of this lack of awareness, difficulties might impact and shape teachers' pedagogical repertoire. A disposition of openness towards pedagogical repertoires focused primarily on adult learners' needs is therefore required by adult educators in order to address difficulties and to self-examine their practices. This is particularly relevant when introducing a change of practices in adult learning, because the adult learners need an appropriate amount of time to ponder on their own world and the usefulness of their connections to the less familiar world of the new learnings (see the Redman and James chapter in this book).

Educators have key roles in helping adult learners to develop their capabilities in recognising their own frames of reference as well as others (Mezirow, 1997). To do so, adult educators can assist learners in participating effectively in conversations that promote reflection and the use of imagination to pose and redefine problems from diverse perspectives. Beliefs and assumptions might be challenged, too, and new interpretations of the world might arise. Likewise, other studies have shown that opening spaces for reflecting on practice can be nurturing for further reflection and this is especially important for monitoring adult learners in the transition between educational programmes and the field of practice. In general terms, instructional materials that reflect real-life experiences of the adult learners can be suggested, as group projects, role play, case studies, simulations, as well as participation in small-group discussions to assess reasons, examine evidence with the purpose of arriving at a reflexive judgement (Higgs, Barnett, Billett, Hutchings and Trede, 2012).

Reflective writing has also been used to enhance reflective practice (Boud, 2001; Bolton, 2005). Writing reflective journals is based on learning from experience, and any attempt to promote new learning must take this experience into account (Boud, 2001). The exercise of writing journals can take place in anticipation of an event, when the event is occurring, or afterwards. The emphasis is on what individuals can do to make the most of events, and journal writing helps to clarify questions that learners need to address in relation to an event (what to do/not to do, what is needed to know to make the event productive and so forth); thus, journals might enhance imaginary scenarios. Indeed, as Gibson, Holme and Taylor mention in their chapter in this book, the actions adult learners perform are imbricated with attitudes, knowledge and reflection.

Pelliccione and Raison (2009) structured a writing journal as a reflective tool based on individual e-portfolios and tested its impact on first year student teachers' reflections. The researchers mapped the progress of student teachers by incorporating each year more structured guides for the reflection process. The results showed higher order reflection increased throughout years, and reflections were more structured and presented in a more coherent manner, as well as showing a better balance between descriptive, analytic appraising and validating comments.

Also in the context of teacher education, but with a different purpose, Cabello and Topping (2014) developed an intervention based on formative peer assessment with final-year student teachers learning to construct explanations about scientific concepts for the classroom. They performed interchangeably as teachers or pupils, mutually gave feedback in a simulated micro-teaching frame and critically reflected on their practice. The results showed they improved their practice in various elements, such as clarity of the explanation, usage of non-verbal resources and connection of the explanation with simulated pupils' ideas. Authors concluded feedback was not the only element encouraging movements in the participants' practice of explaining, but two psychosocial processes enhanced the changes: projection and reflection. When participants took the role of assessors they projected their own decision-making on the peer performance and the participant performing the role of teacher reflected what the assessors would do in a similar teaching situation.

Another example for promoting reflective practices in adult learning is offered by Shaw (2013), who works as a mentor of adult learners in a community learning and development programme. Shaw found strong views that reflection was not part of the adult learners' culture in growing-up or in their previous jobs or experiences, nor was valued in their workplaces. Although a lack of confidence was felt by the adult learners' at the beginning, those who used reflection to evaluate their practice over the years encountered success in reflective writing. Their confidence grew, showing that an awareness of self was an important factor in developing reflection. This is because reflection involves thinking about positives and negatives, along with thinking about the self and what part the self has to play in the situation and the reflective practice. In the final stages of this journey, adult learners became more self-aware and began to assess their own practice and make changes. The latter was enhanced by a change of perspective or frame of reference as Mezirow (1997) argued, because they questioned the elements of their practice, such as their own skills or the character of their workplace.

## Conclusions and recommendations for action

Critical reflection allows you as an adult educator to question your own taken-for-granted frames of reference and interrogate them in order to create new interpretations of the world. Such reflection can help adults (both adult educators and adult learners in the wider society) become autonomous agents and responsible thinkers rooted in permanent learning. We suggest, however, that these reflective and deliberative processes are best fed by diverse sources and not only individual reflection, as perhaps Schön's (1983, 1987) framework implied. Recent research has shown that, in this context, both participants and colleagues' feedback are key in constructing new meanings and solutions for problems, as well as in identifying problems in contexts where these are not evident for adult learners.

Systematic reflective processes on teaching and deliberative self-evaluation on the part of both adult educators and adult learners are needed in order to learn from experiences and make explicit tacit knowledge overcome difficulties. This might be especially helpful if you are an adult educator coming new to adult education since you can analyse what has happened during your teaching, mentoring or supervising practices (see the Ellul and Fehring chapter in this book), and see how you managed difficult situations and so learn how to act in future similar occasions. In becoming aware of a problem and in reflecting on it, the sensitive reading of clues coming from participants of a learning situation (the kinds of questions they raise, and any indication of demotivation and distraction in a learning setting, for example) can be helpful to the educator. At the same time, listening to and sharing other colleagues' problems and the ways they deal with them, might help you as an adult educator to discern new courses of action. In other words, reflective teaching practices and an openness towards new pedagogical repertoires need to be conceptualised beyond an individual and be embedded in social interactions and collaboration that involve other education actors (learners and colleagues across the profession). For professional reflection to be fully open and fruitful, the widest range of perspectives and frameworks need to be brought into view.

In order to promote professional learning through reflection, as an adult educator, you can frame your adult learners' questions in terms of their current levels of understanding and develop activities such as writing reflective journals, conducting group projects and case studies, and performing roleplay and simulations. This can be done in face-to-face encounters or peer coaching or even through communication technologies. Through these activities, adult learners can actively engage the concepts presented in the context of their own experiences and can collectively critically assess the new knowledge being created. Additionally, in order to maximise the chance of discovering new perspectives about a problem or situation, it might be fruitful to bring together professionals from diverse background disciplines and even professional settings. Such cross-disciplinary reflection is also more likely to prompt fundamental critique of the assumptions and practices characteristic of a profession as a whole.

When both adult educators and professionals work together and engage and participate in collective reflective learning processes, educational settings become laboratories in which educators, colleagues and learners work together in order to achieve learning goals. The idea of an educational laboratory has its greatest impact when tacit theories and presuppositions are brought out into the open and subjected to rigorous scrutiny, research and, indeed, critique. Furthermore, these tacitly acquired understandings contribute to personal theories of professional identity, hence, they are relevant (as discussed in the Normand and Morriss chapter in this book). Accordingly, professionals need to become not merely reflective practitioners but scholarly and research-oriented practitioners, which implies giving value to self and peer-criticism in its formative purpose.

## Provocation

Reflection can be carried out not only by an individual but also collectively; it might include face-to-face or virtual encounters. The following suggestions/tips will help you as an adult educator create spaces for reflection to pursue learning goals:

- Jointly with the adult learner, set a realistic learning goal to be reachable in a reasonable period of time and preferably distinguishing medium term goals and stages. Write these down in a shared reflective diary or journal.
- While setting a learning goal, both you and your adult learners might reflect on and evaluate strategies to reach that goal. Write them down in the diary, or journal, and check if there has been any progress in every supervision meeting.
- Construct a programme of reading for, say, a six-month period aimed at widening the adult learner's understanding of professional issues and subsequently identify goals or activities that might reflect that wider understanding.
- During the supervision period, devote time to reflect on those elements that have become challenging or were unexpected. If necessary, reallocate strategies to pursue the learning goal. Include these new strategies in the reflective diary/journal, put them into practices and check their progress.
- In between supervisions, you and your adult learners might have access to the shared reflective diaries/journals in which you might write your reflections that could appear after supervision.
- From time-to-time, organise a collective supervision with other adult learners and adult educators so as to share learning goals and triangulate perspectives around challenging situations and new strategies and resources to address unexpected problems. Use role-play, peer assessment, imagery or study cases to prompt discussion.
- Co-write a short article (say 800 words) about your professional learning experience identifying both strengths and weaknesses and suggesting future ways of action.

## References

Bolton, G. (2005). *Reflective practice: Writing and professional development.* London: Sage.

Boud, D. (2001) Promoting journal writing in adult education. *New Directions for Adult and Continuing Education,* 90, 9–17.

Cabello, V. and Topping, K. (2014). Learning how to make scientific concepts explicit in teacher education: A study of student teachers' explanations, their modifiability and transference. *Pensamiento Educativo. Revista de Investigación Educacional Latinoamericana,* 51(2), 86–97.

Ellul, R. and Fehring, H. (2017). In H. Fehring and S. Rodigues. (eds), *Teaching, coaching and mentoring adult learners: Lessons for professionalism and partnership* (pp. 13–23). London: Routledge.

Eraut, M. (1999). *Developing professional knowledge and competence.* Philadelphia: The Falmer Press.

Fook, J. and Gardner, F. (2007). *Practicing critical reflection.* Maidenhead: Open University Press.

Gibson, C., Holme, R. and Taylor, N. (2017). Professionalism in education. In H. Fehring and S. Rodrigues. (eds), *Teaching, coaching and mentoring adult learners: lessons for professionalism and partnership* (pp. 45–59). London: Routledge.

Guzmán-Valenzuela, C. and Barnett, R. (2013). Developing self-understanding in pedagogical stances: Making explicit the implicit among new lecturers. *Educação e Pesquisa*, 39 (4), 891–906.

Higgs, J., Barnett, R., Billett, S., Hutchings, M. and Trede, F. (eds.). (2012). *Practice-based education: Perspectives and strategies.* Rotterdam, The Netherlands: Sense Publishers.

Hogan, T., Rabinowitz, M. Y. and Craven, J. (2003). Representation in teaching: Inferences from research of expert and novice teachers. *Educational Psychologist*, 38 (4), 235–247.

Knight, P. (2006). *El Profesorado de educación superior. Formación para la excelencia* (2ª edición). Madrid: Narcea.

Lave, J. and Wenger, E. (1991). *Situated learning: Legitimate peripheral participation.* Cambridge: Cambridge University Press.

McAlpine, L., Weston, C., Beauchamp, C., Wiseman, C. and Beauchamp, J. (1999). Building a metacognitive model of reflection. *Higher Education*, 37 (2), 105–131.

Mezirow, J. (1997) Transformative learning: Theory to practice. *New Directions for Adult and Continuing Education*, 74, 5–12.

Normand, C. and Morriss, M. (2017). Professional identity: Insights, strategies and approaches. In H. Fehring and S. Rodrigues. (eds). *Teaching, coaching and mentoring adult learners: Lessons for professionalism and partnership* (pp. 24–34). London: Routledge.

Phelps, L. W. (1991). Practical wisdom and the geography of knowledge in composition. *College English*, 53 (8), 863–885.

Pelliccione, L. and Raison, G. (2009). Promoting the scholarship of teaching through reflecting e-portfolios in teacher education. *Journal of Education for Teaching: International research and pedagogy*, 35 (3), 271–281.

Polanyi, M. (1966). *The tacit dimension.* New York: Doubleday.

Redman, C. and James, D. (2017). Shared objectives and communication. In H. Fehring and S. Rodrigues. (eds), *Teaching, coaching and mentoring adult learners: Lessons for professionalism and partnership* (pp. 99–109). London: Routledge.

Schön, D. A. (1983). *The reflective practitioner: How professionals think in action.* London: Temple Smith.

Schön, D. A. (1987). *Educating the reflective practitioner: Toward a new design for teaching and learning in the professions.* San Francisco: Jossey-Bass.

Shaw, R. (2013). A model of the transformative journey into reflexivity: An exploration into students' experiences of critical reflection. *Reflective Practice*, (14) 3, 319–335

Taylor, C. (2007). *Modern social imaginaries.* Durham, NC: Duke University.

Wenger, E. (1999). *Communities of practice: Learning, meaning, and identity.* Cambridge: Cambridge University Press.

Chapter 4

# Professionalism in adult education

*Carl Gibson, Richard Holme and Neil Taylor*

This chapter considers the notion of adult educators as professionals; explores the notion of professional development as an aspect of being 'professional'; reviews models of learning which can support effective professional development; considers the neuroscience supporting learning approaches; and prompts readers to consider what model of Continuing Professional Development (CPD) best fits their personal and professional development.

## Professionalism and education

The discussion around education, and adult teaching, as a profession is nothing new, as this extract from a paper from the late nineteenth century suggests:

> There are three principal marks of a profession: that it should be a permanent calling taken up as a life-work; that it should require special and intellectual training; and that there should be among members a feeling of common interest and some organization. When we attempt to apply these criteria to the teachers there is certainly some doubt whether we form a profession or no[t].
> (Hart, 1893, pp. 6–7)

Within the education sector, up until the mid-1990s professional development, or in-service training (INSET) was undertaken by educators on a voluntary basis (Craft, 2000) and would often focus on practical skills, subject knowledge, or the introduction of a new initiative. In the UK this would often be facilitated by local government officers or school leadership staff. In some cases, this resulted in a hierarchical approach to professional development, which may have limited the degree to which individuals were able to fulfil their developmental potential. It is clear that the relationship between professionalism and professional development is an important one for adult educators. In this chapter theoretical models of professional development are considered before considering practical applications for mentors and coaches.

Chapter 3 highlights the importance of reflection. As an adult educator you may wish to consider what is meant by the term professional. To assist with your reflection use the list provided below to consider which characteristics would apply to you and your adult learners as professionals.

### Analysis of characteristics of being a professional

- Team working skills
- Dress code or uniform
- Pay level
- Technical knowledge
- Ability to be reflective
- Research skills
- Minimum time in post
- Integrity
- Resilience
- Personal responsibility
- Enthusiasm
- Technical skills
- Working to a set number of hours
- Accountability
- Ensure safety of students
- Follow direct orders
- Represent the interests of government
- Being an expert
- Adhering to a formal set of standards
- Respect others' wishes
- Engagement with professional development
- Flexibility
- Being an expert practitioner
- Time taken to qualify
- Managerial responsibility
- Level of qualification

## Formal standards for educators

The role of adult educator may be applicable within a huge range of professions and careers. Depending on the specific sector there may be statutory requirements that apply within a country or region but there may also be formal standards, which must be adhered to by the employee, and these may require validation by an accrediting body. For example, school-based educators may have a set of professional standards they must follow to allow them to work in that particular sector or setting. When working as a mentor or coach it is essential that you are aware of these standards so you can facilitate your students in achieving these.

As an adult educator it is worth identifying which, if any, formal standards apply to you and reflect on the impact this would have when working with adult learners as an educator or mentor. You may then want to think about the possible conflict that may arise if your adult learners are finding it difficult to adhere to one of the standards.

Earlier in this chapter you as an adult educator had the opportunity to consider your view of what makes someone a professional and how you may support someone to develop in this area. We will now consider some of the academic literature and theoretical concepts that link professionalism to professional development.

### Activity: Analysis of challenges fulfilling a professional standard

*Example: Be able to work collaboratively with stakeholders to uphold the reputation of the profession*

For your personal setting consider what this standard may mean to you as an adult educator and what it means for your adult learners. Think of an example of how this standard might not be met.

What action would be taken to address this issue? Ensure this is clear and action focused (it may include reference to professional reading, an opportunity to shadow fellow professionals, undertaking further formal study or another relevant action).

## Theoretical view of professionalism and the link to professional development

We consider a specific model of professional development (Evans, 2014) in order to help you as an adult educator to analyse and plan your own professional development. Professionalism has often been closely linked to professional development and in recent years this has been explored in greater theoretical depth (see Chapter 2). Evans (2008) defines professionalism as:

> Work practice that is consistent with commonly-held consensual delineations of a specific profession or occupation and that both contribute to and reflects perceptions of the profession's or occupation's purpose and status and the specific nature, range and levels of service provided by, and expertise prevalent within, the profession or occupation, as well as the general ethical code underpinning this practice.
>
> (Evans, 2008, p. 29)

Evans (2014) identified three key elements of professionalism. These are behavioural (relating to the actual practical actions educators engage with), attitudinal (reflecting perceptions, beliefs and values, and motivations of the professional) and intellectual (comprising of practitioner knowledge, and how the individual understands her/his own knowledge structures). To support adult learners with their professional development effectively you should have a sound comprehension of these three categories. The way in which this impacts on professional development is considered next.

## The importance of professional development

Before considering how best you can support the professional development of others it is worth considering why professional development is required at all. It could be argued that fulfilling the statutory requirements of a role or profession is sufficient and additional ongoing development is therefore not required. In addition, trying to prove the efficacy of professional development is also undoubtedly challenging.

## Theoretical models of professional development

The reason for having models of professional development is justified by Evans (2014) as they allow educators to focus development activity for adult learners. Furthermore, this is seen as a complex area and can be oversimplified (Clarke and Hollingsworth, 2002).

Traditional programmes, or models, of professional development in school-based education, usually focus on the practical issue and mechanisms of delivery. Other characteristics of traditional, and incidentally less successful, professional development may be one-off sessions (Clarke and Hollingsworth, 2002) or a model where 'in-service training was done to people rather than being done *with* them' (Boyd, 2005, p. 33). Similarly, professional development can be classed as transmissive (often used in coaching), transitional, or transformative (Kennedy, 2005). By moving the developmental focus from transmissive to transformative allows for greater 'capacity for teacher autonomy' (Kennedy, 2005, p. 248). On a practical level this classification system can be used to analyse the form of professional development being planned or organised by an individual or organisation. This is of particular relevance to a coach or mentor and planning opportunities that are transformative should be seen as a priority.

The componential structure of professionalism discussed earlier (Evans, 2014) can also be applied to professional development. This model aims to reflect, more accurately, the multidimensionality and micro-level developmental nature of professional learning and professional development. This is essential for you

### Activity

Here is some information to help you analyse a professional development activity which you attended as a participant.

***Professional development (PD) activity evaluation (as a participant)***

Provide the name, description, location of PD activity:

- What were the formal aims, objectives, or goals of the PD activity?
- Was the activity predominantly transmissive or transformational, and why?
- As a participant how did you react to the transmissive or transformational nature of the professional development activity?
- How might you apply this to future professional development that you plan for your students?

as an adult educator if you want to be certain that elements of professional development are not overlooked. This model comprises of behavioural development (including processual, procedural, productive, and componential change), attitudinal development (including perceptual, evaluative, and motivational change), and intellectual development (including epistemological, rationalistic, comprehensive, and analytical change). Next we will consider how you, as an adult educator, can apply this when devising and planning professional development activity for your adult learners.

## Behavioural, attitudinal and intellectual components of professional development

Within the model introduced above the behavioural dimension includes practical components of your adult educator's practice and it is likely that a majority of professional development activity, which you have experience of, focuses on this particular element (Evans, 2014). It is important that you also consider the other components of professional development. The second dimension of the above model is concerned with the way in which an individual approaches her/his day-to-day job as an educator. This second set of elements is often overlooked as these are more commonly associated with professional learning rather than professional development (Evans, 2014). The third dimension of the model is concerned with elements relating to intellectual development including comprehension and analytical development including how individuals examine or scrutinise their own professional practice (Evans, 2014).

The activity above is intended to help you when planning professional development to include behavioural, attitudinal and intellectual components.

### Activity

***Evaluation of professional development to include behavioural, attitudinal, and intellectual components***

Provide a name and description of a recent professional development activity you were responsible for leading.

List the formal aims, objectives, and goals of activity:

- Where was the opportunity for behavioural development?
- Where was the opportunity for attitudinal development?
- Where was the opportunity for intellectual development?

Identify the most underdeveloped component of professional development (behavioural, attitudinal or intellectual), which will need to be developed further in future.

Provide an explanation of how this will be addressed.

Start by considering a specific recent example of a professional development activity, which you as an adult educator devised and led. You could select something like a one-off Continuing Professional Development (CPD) session which was planned to develop knowledge of a new medical treatment or something longer term and more sustained, and formal such as undertaking a Master's level module in your specialist field.

The third dimension of the Evans' (2014) model relates to intellectual development. Therefore an adult educator that understands how the brain operates during learning can more readily move from merely transferring information to, creating a transformative experience for her/his adult students.

## Neuroscience of professional education development

The substantial exploration of neuroscience and neuropsychology of recent years provides adult educators with essential insight and a powerful set of tools with which to improve their design and delivery of professional development.

Traditional views of the adult brain promote ideas such as: a massive loss of brain cells (in the region of 40%) occurring since childhood; the adult brain being more fixed and rigid (significantly less plastic) with lowered cognitive ability; and less able to learn new complex skills. If all of this was true, this would present a substantial challenge to designing and delivering professional development programmes. Learning in the adult brain relies on multiple cognitive and neural systems, the experience of which generates continuing changes in brain structure and function. Memory formation is at the core of learning and is dependent upon this range of independent neural networks that form and reform in the brain. As neural systems become more specialised into adulthood and expertise becomes embedded, there is some reduction in neural plasticity, and a substantial weakening and pruning of unused neurons and connections as the brain ages. This means that some forms of learning capacity do diminish, for example, short-term working memory. However, broad pattern recognition skills, essential to complex problem solving and abstract thinking, and long-term memory, (particularly declarative – episodic memory) improve in the aging brain.

## Declarative memory

Declarative memory is explicit, is consciously recognised and is the principal form of memory used to encode professional development learning (Rule et al., 2011). Declarative memory is composed of two subsets: semantic memory (remembering facts and lists) and episodic memory (contextual memories). The creation of episodic memory is essential to effective professional development learning as it actively interrelates complex and arbitrarily related concepts, (Ferbinteanu et al., 2006). This, for example, allows the new learning to be placed within a framework of an adult learner's prior knowledge and workplace experience, adapt that prior learning to novel contexts, and apply the integrated learning to solve new complex problems. Furthermore, episodic memory can be triggered from only partial cues (Eichenbaum and Cohen, 2001), allowing learning to be applied in unfamiliar and dynamic contexts, the environment often faced by professionals in the modern workplace.

Memory forms the foundation for learning, and it is important for you as an adult educator to understand how memory is formed, how learning is embedded and how memory is retrieved, thus allowing professional learning to be applied. Memories are not stored away as complete defined containerised 'images' or 'documents'. Rather a 'memory' is stored across multiple neural networks, being re-created afresh each time it is recalled. The way in which the memory is initially embedded along with the manner and frequency of recall can serve to either strengthen or degrade that memory by stimulating neuronal growth and increasing connections between them, or by pruning connections and atrophying neuronal networks (Delazer et al., 2003).

Teaching, mentoring and coaching techniques that promote the formation of these new neural networks and limit the atrophy of other beneficial networks will provide the basis for a robust professional development learning architecture. The application of a number of such techniques is discussed below in subsequent sections of this chapter.

The brain also uses two discrete thinking systems, which will profoundly affect how learning materials are attended to, analysed, and processed for memory formation:

- The analytical thinking system, controlled by the prefrontal cortex, provides conscious reasoning, is deliberative, requires significant focus and attention, and needs significant effort and energy. This allows us to make sense of information, particularly where quantitative analysis is required.
- The emotional thinking system, is far more rapid than the analytical system (which can often be playing catch-up), is automatic, is not under conscious control, and is relatively effortless with low energy demands. The emotional thinking system broadens the learning perspective beyond that provided by the analytical system and can provide a more sophisticated and nuanced appreciation of complex concepts.

Both thinking systems (which also support Evans' (2014) model) are essential to effective learning in professional development contexts and usually work in tandem. However, when the analytical system becomes overburdened (cognitive overload or under adverse stress) its controlling influence over the emotional thinking system is diminished. The emotional system then becomes a dominant driver in thinking and learning, providing shallower quantitative consideration of the teaching materials and introducing unhelpful biases into its analysis. It is therefore important that your professional development activities are structured and delivered in a way that promotes the appropriate balance of the two thinking systems.

Adults engage with teaching materials in a very different way to a child. The experience for a child is foundational, establishing ground truths and needs to be immersive; whereas the experience for the adult learner is more selective, responsive and relational (Knowland and Thomas, 2014), where both the teaching material and interaction between adult educator and adult learners need to engage with and be salient to learners' prior experiences. Given that the majority of those undertaking professional development will have specific individual backgrounds, objectives and expectations, then learning paths in many circumstances will need to be individualised. If you as an adult educator develop individualised learning approaches, based upon both discovery and challenge using multiple sensory inputs, this will help your adult learners to build complex interrelationships between existing and newly formed neural networks. This is vitally important in allowing adult learners to frame their learning in the context of their wider experience and apply it in their professional environment.

## A combined framework for professional development learning

Zull (2006) proposed learning cycles. A revised framework provides a useful iterative learning model comprising:

### *i) Attention and gathering*

One of the limitations of effective learning is poor attention arising from disinterest or distraction. A common aspect of this is the designer/ educator's failure to limit the number of tasks being undertaken at any one time by the adult learner, i.e. the educator has inadvertently promoted multitasking. To a large extent multitasking is a fallacy, and those able to genuinely multitask are exceptionally rare (Strayer and Watson, 2012). When an individual is paying attention to a single task, the prefrontal cortex in both hemispheres are involved and work together on that task (Charron and Koechlin, 2010). When attention is split between two tasks, there is a substantial decrease in learning capability, the prefrontal cortex in each hemisphere work independently, significantly reducing the cognitive resources available and increasing appreciably the error rate. Gaining and maintaining attention requires an engaged prefrontal cortex, too much data and it is rapidly overwhelmed, with restricted processing occurring and a failure to embed key information into longer-term memory. Achieving engagement is a factor of both the:

- Content – its salience to the adult learner's objectives and alignment with past knowledge; and
- Adult educator's ability to deliver a problem-centred approach rather than a subject-centred approach (Merriam, 2011), thereby better stimulating neural connections with pre-existing knowledge.

Furthermore, gathering is subject to very low capacity limits with working memory only holding approximately five to seven 'chunks' of information at any one time, although it could be as low as only four 'chunks' (Cowan, 2010). You as an adult educator need to structure your content and delivery to allow sufficient time for processing information in the working memory and then to transfer it into longer-term memory. Too much sensory input, delivered too rapidly overwhelms adult learners' working memory, reduces their attention and understanding, and impairs long-term memory formation.

An adult learner's emotional status has a profound effect on learning, influencing attention, motivation, approach to learning engagement and strategy (Pekrun, 2014). Keeping their attention can be achieved through a range of techniques, which increase the release of hormones dopamine and norepinephrine. As an adult educator you could try:

- providing a sense of reward (dopamine release), where the adult learner sees the value of the learning that can be achieved. Make the content relatable to and realistic for the adult learner;
- providing novelty (Bunzeck and Duzel, 2006) by using different learning techniques such as case studies (dopamine release);
- reducing fatigue, through improved sleep patterns;
- creating a sense of manageable stress (Rock, 2008) by introducing group simulations which can generate an increased arousal response (norepinephrine);
- developing social interaction by creating a shared narrative;
- increasing intake of L-Tyrosine as part of a balanced healthy diet;
- taking regular aerobic exercise; and
- practising mindfulness techniques.

### *ii) Reflection and spacing*

Reflective practice and reflection have been discussed more comprehensively in Chapter 3. Reflection in professional development involves creating associations with previous knowledge and experience. In the brain this involves making large numbers of new connections between multiple different neural networks. Reflection works best when there are no distractions, when sensory inputs are minimised.

In many forms of teaching as learning becomes consolidated, much of it will be going directly into semantic memory. However, much of professional development learning is framed around the context of previous experience and expertise, forming episodic rather than semantic memory. This requires new neural connections to be generated among diverse pre-existing networks of neurons, a process that requires time for reflection. Thus professional learning that is based around cramming new facts does not provide the opportunity for such reflection, as associations are not created, neural connections are not formed and learning does not become enriched and embedded. Time needs to be made available to allow new synaptic connections to be formed (Goda and Davis, 2003) and consolidation of meaning to occur (Tambini et al., 2010). Generally the longer the period of spacing between sessions the better subsequent retrieval of the learning.

### *iii) Generation and creation*

Where meaning is constructed through narrative it can have greater resonance with the adult learner (see Chapter 8), can carry more meaning, be more readily accessible and be more resilient to error in subsequent recall. The construction of narrative triggers multiple areas of the brain (Siegel, 2012) and integrates a range of neural networks. Narrative appears to utilise areas of the brain that are more resistant to memory loss (for example, through aging) compared with those parts of the brain where more list-based factual information is stored in semantic memory. Narrative also facilitates sharing of information, which in itself can significantly increase creation of meaning, with up to 90% of learning occurring through social interaction (Davachi and Wagner, 2002).

Stress within the learning environment, or external stress affecting the learner can have adverse effects on neural plasticity, hippocampus functioning, and over stimulation of the amygdalae (controlling emotional thinking), which releases various chemicals that reduce attention and adversely affect neural networks. However, too little arousal results in a loss of motivation. This presents you as an adult educator with a bit of a challenge in the design and delivery of professional development to manage the optimal level of arousal or stress.

From a professional development and learning perspective, gaining attention and establishing strong emotional response can be highly dependent upon exposure to ideas and to new people, which will challenge the adult learner's perceptions and understanding of the world. This challenge will create new neuronal connections, restimulate existing connections and provide a structure of complexity that was previously absent (Mezirow, 2000).

## Putting neuroscience into practice

Neuroscience and neuropsychology gives us a unique understanding of how information is captured and manipulated within the brain, why emotional layering is important, how memory is formed and recalled, and how attention and focus are affected by the content, context, narrative and environment. This understanding can provide you as an adult educator with the insight necessary to create a rich and immersive professional development learning experience that can move you and your adult learners from simply teaching and learning to creating sustainable development of deeply embedded professional capabilities. Table 4.1a, b, c summarise the 'neuro' principles and how these can be practically utilised by both you as an adult educator and your adult learners.

*Table 4.1a* Applying 'neuro' principles to educator and student action

*'Neuro' principle – Enhance attention and gathering:*

- Reduce multitasking.
- Increase cognitive processing.
- Activate both hemispheres of the brain to a single task.
- Stimulate both analytical and emotional response.

*Application*

*Adult educator strategies*

- Avoid multitasking learning activities which create distraction.
- Have learning objective clearly aligned to professional development need.
- Stimulate the emotional and cognitive response by framing the learning as a problem to be solved rather than a factual account to be remembered.
- Establish learning context with a framework of the learner's prior experiences.
- Encapsulate the learning experience as a salient shared narrative.

*Adult student strategies*

- Pay attention to fatigue levels and general health to improve attentiveness.
- Be willing to share one's experiences where relevant to the learning objectives.

*Table 4.1b* Applying 'neuro' principles to educator and student action

*'Neuro' principle – Reflection and spacing*

- Stimulate generation of episodic memory.
- Create neural networks linking the new with prior learning and experience.
- Establish the neural architecture for subsequent memory retrieval.

*Application*

*Adult educator strategies*

- Provide time and space to reflect upon their immediate learning experience.
- Demonstrate with examples – what reflection involves and how to practise it.
- Provide opportunities for self-reflection to become consolidated with others.
- Create reflective opportunities as part of 'homework' activities.
- Structure learning to give reflection time between new concepts.

*Adult student strategies*

- Ensure understanding of why reflection is important and how to approach it.
- Treat opportunities for reflection seriously and use time wisely.
- Use reflection to frame new learning in a professional and personal context.
- Use group sessions to establish newly acquired learning into a wider context.

*Table 4.1c* Applying 'neuro' principles to educator and student action

*Neuro principle – Generation and creation*

- Stimulate multiple areas of the brain.
- Create individual meaning and shared sensemaking.
- Build error resistant long term memory.

*(continued)*

*Table 4.1c* (Continued)

*Application*

*Adult educator strategies*

- Create learning opportunities round narrative, (case studies, personal stories, hypotheticals and simulations).
- Create learning narratives that use learners' experiences and knowledge.
- Provide different perspectives to the learners' backgrounds, current beliefs and accepted 'wisdom', particularly where this can be counterintuitive.
- Learn to recognise unmanaged stress.
- Learning must be aimed at changing existing and creating new behaviours.

*Adult student strategies*

- Learn how to cope with increasing stress, reflecting on why the stress is occurring and how you are coping with it.

Use periods of reflection to understand why the new learning is challenging, threatening dearly held beliefs and when necessary be open to adapting these beliefs or even letting them go.

## Practical applications of continuing professional development in education

Professional development is an integral component of what it means to be a professional. Many professions such as medicine, dentistry and law require that practitioners engage in Continuing Professional Development (CPD) if the practitioner wishes to meet the requirements of their professional and regulatory bodies thus enabling them to continue in practice. Many countries have professional bodies regulating the professional standards of their workforce and educators' fitness to practice. In nearly all of these sets of standards a commitment to professional development is a fundamental responsibility of the educator.

To support effective teacher professional development Darling-Hammond and McLaughlin (1995) suggest that CPD should encompass three domains. The domains include:

- opportunities for teacher enquiry and collaboration;
- strategies to reflect teachers' questions and concerns; and
- access to successful models of (new) practice (p. 2).

A pertinent question is how can adult educators who are geographically distant from colleagues engage in collaborative critical enquiry and peer support? There is a growing use of web 2.0 tools deployed by educators locally, nationally and internationally to support their professional development. There also appears to be an unstated assumption that educators (and especially younger practitioners) will happily collaborate and share in online environments. However, is this the case? (For more information see Chapter 7). Recently there has been a proliferation of release of Massive Open Online Courses (MOOCs) and other Open

Educational Resources (OERs). There is also in some cases the option to attain recognised credit for the study or use the learning to gain 'badges' as recognition of engagement in the learning. Many of these MOOCs provide online support from tutors and peer support via blogs and discussion forums. Why are educators not fully availing themselves of these professional learning opportunities? As an adult educator contemplating these models of CPD and in light of your understanding of the functioning of the brain described in this chapter why do you think the attrition rates are so high? If you had enrolled on any such course and did not complete it what were your reasons for stopping your studies? How could you as an adult educator help your adult learners to overcome these challenges?

In times of tightening financial resource and greater demands being made of adult educators what are the potential benefits to you of MOOCs and OERs? In what ways can you or have you used such resources to support your practice and enhance your adult students' learning?

It is clear that professional learning is a fundamental expectation for all adult educators and that effective CPD has moved on from 'top tips for educators' to a more reflective and research-informed activity. Consideration has to be given to how best to enable adult educators to collaborate in a time of challenging financial constraints as the cost of 'face-to-face' CPD may become too great. However, not all practitioners are comfortable collaborating in a digital space. There also has to be consideration of how to recognise the informal professional learning that adult educators engage in such as Teachmeets etc. Collaboration is seen as key. CPD opportunities which give educators time to research new methodologies, reflect on this learning, and carry out small action-research projects in collaboration with others is more likely to have the greatest impact on their practice and hence the adult learner's experiences.

## Provocation

As an adult educator:

1. Revisit your own experiences of professional learning. Which model of professional development best suited you and why did it suit you?
2. What do you perceive to be the challenges to engaging in critical evaluation of other adults' work and/or have your comments and work critically reviewed by others? What skills do you think are required to collaborate effectively in an online community? Develop an audit in order to ascertain which skills you think you may need to develop.
3. Given the need for accountability for professional learning how would you evidence the impact of your professional learning in terms of the impact on the adult learners and on yourself as an adult educator?

## References

Boyd, B. (2005). *CPD: Improving professional practice: An introduction to CPD for teachers.* Paisley: Hodder Gibson.

Bunzeck, N. and Duzel, E. (2006). Absolute coding of stimulus novelty in the human substantia nigra/VTA. *Neuron*, 51(3), 369–379.

Clarke, D. and Hollingsworth, H. (2002). Elaborating a model of teacher professional growth. *Teaching and Teacher Education*, 18, 947–967.

Charron, S. and Koechlin, E. (2010). Divided representation of concurrent goals in the human frontal lobes. *Science*, 328(360), 360–363.

Cowan, N. (2010). The magical mystery four: How is working memory capacity limited, and why? *Current Directions in Psychological Science*, 19(1), 51–57.

Craft, A. (2000). *Continuing professional development: A practical guide for teachers and schools.* London: RoutledgeFalmer.

Darling-Hammond, L. and McLaughlin, M. W. (1995). Policies that support professional development in an era of reform. *Phi Delta Kappan*, 76(8), 597–604.

Davachi, L. and Wagner, A. D. (2002). Hippocampal contributions to episodic encoding: Insights from relational and item-based learning. *The American Physiological Society*, 88, 982–990.

Delazer, M., Domahs, F., Bartha, L., Brenneis, C., Lochy, A., Trieb, T. and Benke, T. (2003). Learning complex arithmetic – an fMRI study. *Cognitive Brain Research*, 18, 76–88.

Eichenbaum, H. E. and Cohen, N. J. (2001). *From conditioning to conscious recollection: Memory systems of the brain.* New York: Oxford University Press.

Evans, L. (2008). Professionalism, professionality and the development of education professionals. *British Journal of Educational Studies*, 56, 20–38. (Avaliable via http://www.tandfonline.com/doi/abs/10.1080/13674580701292913 Accessed 09 December 2015)

Evans, L. (2014). Leadership for professional development and learning: Enhancing our understanding of how teachers develop. *Cambridge Journal of Education*, 44(2), 179–198.

Ferbinteanu, J., Kennedy, P. J. and Shapiro, M. L. (2006). Episodic memory – from brain to mind. *Hippocampus*, 16, 691–703.

Goda, Y. and Davis, G. W. (2003). Mechanisms of synapse assembly and disassembly. *Neuron*, 40(2), 243–264.

Hart, A. B. (1893). The teacher as a professional expert. *The School Review*, 1, 4–14.

Kennedy, A. (2005). Models of continuing professional development: A framework for analysis. *Journal of In-Service Education*, 31, 235–250.

Knowland, V. C. P. and Thomas, M. S. C. (2014). Educating the adult brain: How the neuroscience of learning can inform educational policy. *International Review of Education*, 60, 99–122.

Merriam, S. B. (2011). Adult learning. In Rubenson K. (ed.), *Adult learning and education*, pp. 29–34. Oxford: Academic Press.

Mezirow, J. (2000). *Learning as transformation: Critical perspectives on a theory in progress.* San Francisco, CA: Jossey-Bass.

Pekrun, R. (2014). Emotions in learning. *Educational Practices Series* 24. International Academy of Education, Brussels, Belgium and International Bureau of Education, Geneva, Switzerland.

Rock, D. (2008). SCARF: a brain-based model for collaborating with and influencing others. *NeuroLeadership Journal*, 1, 1–7.

Rule, M., Rock, D. and Donde, R. (2011). *Global coaching study* 2011, NeuroLeadership Group, Sydney.

Siegel, D. J. (2012). *The developing mind: How relationships and the brain interact to shape who we are,* Second edition. New York: Guilford Press.

Strayer, D. L. and Watson, J. M. (2012). Supertaskers and the multi-tasking brain. *Scientific American Mind*, March–April 2012, 22–29.

Tambini, A., Ketz, N. and Davachi, L. (2010). Enhanced brain correlations during rest are related to memory for recent experiences. *Neuron*, 65, 280–282.

Teachmeets (Available via http://teachmeet.pbworks.com/w/page/19975349/FrontPage Accessed May 2015).

Zull, J. E. (2006). Key aspects of how the brain learns. *New Directions for Adult and Continuing Education*, 110, 3–7.

Chapter 5

# Including adult learners from diverse cultural backgrounds

*Owen Barden, William Youl and Eva Janice Youl*

## Introduction

Imagine fluently speaking two languages, but not English, and having two degrees from Cairo University, and then having to retrain in a new language – English. This is the example of a teacher, who we will call E, from Egypt, a Coptic Christian, who managed to emigrate to Australia just before the Arab Spring political uprising in January 2011. Her husband came to Australia on a skilled immigrant visa. E's qualifications were not recognised in Australia, so she had to retrain. E's story is but one of a number from adult students in Australia and the United Kingdom. We obtained these stories by interview, and we use them in this chapter with a view to illustrating how you as an adult educator can help international adult students. In relaying these students' voices, we attempt to re-emphasise the importance of mentors, coaches and tutors understanding the principles underpinning inclusiveness.

In this chapter we look at cultural aspects of inclusive education. Whereas 'inclusion' is often taken only to refer to disabled students, or those deemed to have 'special needs', in this chapter we use it in a broader sense, encompassing learners whose needs arise at least in part from their diverse cultural backgrounds. Adult educators increasingly find themselves working with students from diverse cultural backgrounds, some of whom will also be disabled. Psychological factors such as trauma, and socioeconomic factors such as poverty, further impact on students' education and opportunities. We present evidence of some such adult learners' educational experiences, and use it to argue that it is imperative that you as an adult educator understand the cultural backgrounds of your students, and the wider global context, in striving to provide inclusive adult education.

## Inclusion in adult education

There is no easy or universally agreed definition of 'inclusion', but one way of thinking about it is the attempt to make education accessible and meaningful for all, with everybody learning together with and from each other (Hart et al., 2004). Historically, education systems in the Western world have tended to separate and segregate different learners groups on the basis of factors such as class, gender, race and disability. In contrast, to educate inclusively means to give everybody equitable access to education, irrespective of these perceived differences. The growth of inclusive education has been prompted in part by increased recognition of human diversity, and of educators' social and moral obligation to educate everybody (Hodkinson and Vickerman, 2009). Yet there has always been a pragmatic motivation for inclusion, as countries have adapted their education systems – in response to increased socio-cultural diversity, brought about by factors including the end of colonialism and greater labour-force mobility – to try and promote social cohesion as well as economic productivity (Armstrong et al., 2010). Bouchard (2006) explains that although individuals may enhance their earning capacity through continuing education, there is a threat to the idea of education as an inherently valuable thing, and that human capital and the knowledge economy become mere trappings for neoliberal political agendas. 'The more the concept of "lifelong learning" becomes synonymous with market requirements, the more it becomes commodified, and alienated from the learner' (Bouchard, 2006, p. 166).

Students who are disabled, who are educationally or economically disadvantaged, or who are immigrants (and some adult learners will be all three) can often be frustrated in their attempts to participate in continuing education because they are made to feel different and inadequate by their classmates and teachers, lack the information and support they need to be successful, struggle financially, or do not understand what their teachers or institutions want from them. These financial, institutional and social barriers may well serve to further alienate adult students who would otherwise be highly motivated learners (Bowl, 2001).

Therefore, it is vital to keep the adult learner as the focus, and for adult education to provide opportunities for meaningful learning and civic participation for today's diverse populations (Hyland and Merrill, 2003).

## Methodology

Some years ago, Owen Barden conducted research in a large Further Education (FE) College in North-West England, which was commissioned by the Learning and Skills Development Agency (a now-defunct FE quality assurance body) in response to new anti-discriminatory legislation, the Disability Discrimination Act Part IV. In this UK study (LSDA, 2004) 12 one-to-one interviews were conducted with disabled students from minority ethnic backgrounds. A focus group was also conducted with a group of BME (black and minority ethnic) tutor/mentors who underwent training at the College. This provided an opportunity for a wide range of views to be expressed and for emergent issues to be explored in greater depth. As an adult educator it is important to try and get a sense of your adult learners' personal, family and community backgrounds, what they perceive as the barriers to inclusive education, as well as their ideas of what makes for good educational practice.

In Australia, four adult students were interviewed in 2015. These students all had different language backgrounds and were studying different courses at four post-school institutions, with a view to changing careers. The interview questions were similar to those asked in the UK, and based on suggestions for best practice. The selected transcript excerpts provided in this chapter to illustrate our themes are all from these Australian students.

Despite the two phases of data collection taking place several years apart, and on different continents, striking similarities in adult learners' experiences became apparent. This again underscores the importance of you, as an adult educator, needing to prioritise inclusive thinking in your reflection and practice. Four themes emerged from the Australian data: motivation, obstacles, learning preferences and what makes a good educator. These themes are relevant to the adult educator's understanding of the adult learner.

## Motivation

What is the common motivational force for adults returning to higher education or entering for the first time? It is widely accepted that mature students are highly motivated and keen to do well (Frumkin and Koutsoubou, 2013). This may mean that mature age students put too much pressure on themselves by trying for a high grade for every piece of work. Most Australian adult learners in our study wished to further their careers, to increase their salary, change to a new career or, as in the case of student T, improve themselves. He was nearing completion of his degree and had gained outstanding results.

> Most of the students in my classes are straight from school. I am not there for my career or for making money. I had my own business, which I sold and I am still a minority shareholder. I did not finish high school and this has been a regret because I think I am reasonably smart. So I decided to do Spanish at a TAFE college – Certificate 4 Course in Spanish – so that I could enjoy travel more. I couldn't enrol at my current university until I had completed the certificate course (3 years). The university has an arrangement with a university near Florence where I also studied before being accepted.
>
> My motivation was proving to myself that I could do it. So I am doing a Bachelor of Arts with a major in Italian Studies. I am doing this part-time with generally two units per semester.

In contrast, student J who is Australian-born but who speaks Vietnamese at home has followed his parents' example and aspirations and worked very hard to achieve his academic qualification. He supplements his finances by working as a barista in a cafe. He decided he wanted a career change. Money is not the motivation; it is the work he wants to do that prompted the career change.

> I am Vietnamese but born in Australia, so I am Australian. I speak Vietnamese at home, more Vietnamese than English, because my parents speak broken English. I try and go back to Vietnam every year just to be exposed to the language again.
>
> I finished VCE and did my first degree in Marketing in 2000 and finished in 2003. This was at ... university. I think if I had done a gap year after Year 12 I would have done something else.
>
> These days we have a lot of opportunities to do whatever we like, so I decided to move away from Marketing and try something new. I am a cyclist and have been injured and that is when I became interested in myotherapy.
>
> I am studying a Bachelor of Health Science majoring in muscular skeletal at College X in the city. I still have HECS (Higher Education Contribution Scheme) left and it is going to cost me $47,000.
>
> I think it's a lot easier going back to study as an adult. I think you are more focused and have more life experiences. The students in my group are half just finished secondary school and half are adults, mature and also some elderly students.

The reduction of government support for universities, Technical and Further Education (TAFE)/Vocational Education (VE) in Australia and other adult education organisations, including the Skills Funding Agency in England, has led to private education providers increasing their active recruitment of foreign students. This means you as an adult educator in this field are likely to encounter increased cultural diversity in your classrooms, and with it a range of motivations. For example, in contrast to student T and student J, student C is tapping into the financial boom of property in Melbourne and Sydney. In our assessment of the conversation, student C's motivation is for financial gain, but cultural nuances mean student C would not state this outright.

> First, I study in Sydney for accounting and actuarial profession ... and then I go back to China and work as an actuary for two years. Then I decide I would like to move back to Australia with my wife and study in Melbourne.
>
> I found it difficult to get job in this area, so I am now doing a Master of Property at University... I am currently full-time student but if I find a job I will go part-time. Fortunately I get some exemptions so I will not pay the full cost of the degree, which is over $47k.

What is often forgotten when talking about teaching and learning is that they are fundamentally about relationships. The best pedagogical strategies in the world are useless without good student–teacher relationships. Thus as an adult educator taking the time to understand adult students' cultural backgrounds and motivations, and thereby establishing a positive and informed relationship is an important aspect of educating inclusively.

## Obstacles

As well as motivations, it helps for you as an adult educator to be aware of the barriers culturally diverse students face. Among numerous others, adult learners face language difficulties, financial struggles and competing demands, especially if studying part-time. Trauma also affects many refugees and it impacts on their ability to study.

### *Language*

Students C and E highlight the language issues many face. For EAL (English as an Additional Language) adult learners, any new learning environment where L1 (the student's first language) is not used can create confusion. Student C appears to have the biggest language barrier, and explained that small group discussion was good because of the high proportion of Chinese-speaking students in the classes.

> Adult learning environment is similar to learning in China. The main difference is the communication, which can be too fast or not clear. Small group discussion is OK.

Student E, who we introduced at the start of our chapter, overcame her own EAL (English as an Additional Language) language barrier by using her own children as language support. She had one child who was at university and another in the penultimate year of secondary school in Australia. Her statement illustrates the use of close family being part of her support network, along with her tutor and other official sources.

> The course was not easy and I found I was struggling with assignments because of my language. I had to present in front of my classmates. My mentor at AMES (Australian Migrant Education Services) was very supportive...yes my family was supportive.... my husband helped at home. My children helped me with assignments, translating hard words.

Other adult learners also emphasised the importance of family support:

> My partner finished her degree two years ago.... she reads my work because her English is better than mine. I also have had good support from work, especially if I have an assignment or exam. (Student J)

Opportunities for adult learners to use L1 (first language) and recognition of an adult educator's role in adult learners' support networks would thus seem to be components of inclusive education for adult learners from diverse cultural backgrounds. Although we cannot expect you as an adult educator to be proficient in every language you might encounter in your classroom, there are still things you can do to address language barriers. As noted above, you as an adult educator could provide opportunities for small group discussions in the adult learners' first languages if there were sufficient numbers in the class. Alternatively, adult learners could be encouraged to set up study groups where they could work in their own language; adult learners could be encouraged to work informally in their own language, for example by blogging or via social networks; organisations could foster opportunities for families to work together in drop-in study sessions or outreach work. All these offer opportunities for adult learners to reflect on and hence deepen their learning. The principles of Universal Design for Learning (UDL), outlined below, may also help address some aspects of the language barriers faced by EAL adult learners.

### *Competing demands*

Although financial hardship is a barrier to many adult learners, especially young adults in the age group 18–25, our interviewees were not forthcoming about financial hardship. Speaking to a student councillor in Victoria, Australia, adult learners are often fatigued because they are studying and holding down casual jobs in cafes or retail. In Australia international students face part-time work restrictions on student visas during semesters, which can result in financial stress. These factors suggest that you as an adult educator need to be aware of the financial, study support and pastoral services available to adult learners in order to be able to advise them appropriately. Where possible, you should also be prepared to work flexibly, for example in the arrangement of workloads and assessment deadlines.

### *Cultural differences*

As well as financial pressures, cultural differences can also create barriers and a sense of isolation. In the UK-based interviews, both disabled and non-disabled Sudanese students said they were confused by differing expectations of disabled people: they were shocked that British society expected them to be as independent as possible when, for example, getting around the campus or trying to access public transport. In contrast, in their home country people would have been expected to go out of their way to offer help. Induction, familiarisation and orientation activities that enable adult learners to safely share their culture, prior experiences and concerns, while also giving adult educators opportunities to explain the expectations on students and relevant aspects of the host culture could help address these issues, as well as providing another opportunity for relationship-building.

### *Trauma*

Adult learners who are refugees in a new country face further obstacles when returning to learning for re-establishment purposes. In addition to language, finances and housing issues, adult refugee students who have experienced trauma and injuries and are now living with psychological and/or physical impairments perhaps require support and understanding the most.

Refugee background children and young people must make a series of transitions through the education system. This is a challenge on a number of levels. To begin with, it is likely that all refugee background children and young people have had either disrupted educational experiences or, in some cases, no education at all. *The Refugee Resettlement Handbook* states that 'Schools are one of the first casualties of war' (United Nations High Commission for Refugees, 2002, p. 23). Adult educators and the education system itself may have been specifically targeted for elimination in the conflicts that lead to refugee flight. 'Additionally, refugees may have limited entitlement to education in their countries of asylum' (VFST, 2011, p. 15).

The Victorian Foundation for Survivors of Torture (VFST, also known as Foundation House) resource booklet gives an overview of the refugee challenges. The document explains what refugees have gone through and how this affects their well-being and ability to learn. Again, an informed empathetic approach, knowledge of support services and mechanisms, and flexibility are key in addressing these issues.

### *Learning preferences*

We know that different adult learners have different preferences and strengths in the ways they learn. Although the idea of individual students having reliably identifiable 'learning styles' has now been largely discredited, it is recognised that adult educators do have a duty to maximise learning opportunities for their adult learners through flexible, relevant pedagogy (Coffield et al., 2004). Cultural background and learning preferences can be interrelated and also play a part in creating a more inclusive environment. Refugees from the Horn of Africa, for example, have an oral tradition and do not necessarily rely on reading books to the same extent as other learners: historically, most African societies did not have a written alphabet, meaning oral and musical traditions were of greater significance. Having adult teaching staff who are knowledgeable about adult learners' cultural backgrounds has been shown to increase feelings of inclusion (Frumkin and Koutsoubou, 2013). Meanwhile, greater access to technology (see Chapter 7) is affording more opportunities for you as an adult educator to design inclusively, and for adult learners to work according to their strengths and preferences. As well as offering opportunities to work in L1 and recognising your role in adult learners' support networks, you as tutor, mentor and coach can maximise learning opportunities by following the principles of Universal Design for Learning (UDL). These include (CAST, 2012):

- **Equitable design** of curriculum and materials, so that they are useful to all people (see Chapter 6), e.g. giving information in a range of formats including oral and written language as well as through symbols and visuals.
- **Flexibility** to accommodate a broad range of abilities and preferences, e.g. choice of assessment methods – class project or individual work.
- **Simple, intuitive** instructions and information, perceptible to all.
- **Tolerance of error** – for example, giving opportunities for formative feedback before any high-stakes assessment.
- **A community of learners** where the tutor models a welcoming, inclusive attitude and promotes interaction between students.

Student J's comment highlights how learning is done in different ways, partly according to the nature of what is being learned, partly curriculum design, and partly individual preference and technology availability:

> The younger generation bring in their laptops. They are always typing in class. I like to write it out first as that helps it go into my head. For revision I will read it again but if it is practical work it will just stay in my head. For example if I am learning a stretch, then by doing it, it will just stay in my head.
>
> Earlier there was 50/50 for theory and practical, and now in my final year, 75% is practical. My science subjects are online. You do have an option to have face-to-face or do it online.

## What makes a good educator of adults?

The adult learners interviewed reinforced what we all know: a teacher, coach, supervisor or mentor needs to be knowledgeable and enthusiastic about her/his area of expertise. The earlier chapters of this book refer to good practice and the work of Malcolm Knowles (1980). In Knowles' *The Modern Practice of Adult Education*, he identifies a list of Conditions of Learning and related Principles of Teaching. The condition most relevant to this chapter is 'The learning environment is characterised by physical comfort, mutual trust and respect, mutual helpfulness, freedom of expression, and acceptance of differences' (Knowles, 1980, p. 57). This sentiment is echoed in the principles for UDL listed above. The Centre for Multicultural Youth (CMY) (2015), based in Melbourne, has produced short videos available on YouTube called 'Tips for Tutors'. The video on Communication Skills has the following summary dot points:

- be patient, friendly, respectful;
- use a variety of approaches;

- focus on the positives;
- ensure student-led sessions.

We asked our Australian adult learners what made a good educator, and they identified similar characteristics to those listed above. They also appeared to be more discerning, even critical, of their tutors, as can be seen in the quotes below. The quotes emphasise the importance of you as an adult educator getting to know your adult learners and their preferences.

Student J is qualifying in a new area of Health Science because of his interest in myotherapy. He emphasised an imperative for lecturers to have worked in the field. He was scathing of one lecturer who did not know his field.

> Teachers who have worked in the field have a lot more knowledge. With this type of course, it is important that the teacher has worked in the field. If the teacher has not worked in the field I can see when they make a mistake. I have worked in the field and so I can tell if they make a mistake… . Yes I do correct them.
>
> I know it is not right and the teacher is not sure. I am an adult and I am paying for the course!
>
> A key attribute of a good lecturer is that they know the field and have worked in the area.

Student C was concerned about the communication skills of the lecturer. There are not any pre-requisites for the Master of Property, so Student C was alarmed when a lecturer from industry assumed that the students had a strong background in construction and planning.

> The lecturer must be speaking clearly. The notes that come with the lecture are important. A good teacher needs to be a good communicator and needs to give an overall plan. Sometimes we are confused about where the lecturer is going.
>
> Yes the lecturer needs to be interested in the subject. We have two academics and one lecturer who are from industry. This is the one where we have difficulty. She is not good at teaching.

Student T, who was 62 years old, had many accumulated life experiences to add to his perspective. This may be a factor in his high expectations. He was very definite about what he wanted. He was also critical of a university lecturer in French, and had made a written complaint.

> All the lecturers are different. Some are really good. The teaching style is important for me. We know that having a PhD does not make you a good lecturer.

> A good lecturer is someone who captures your interest, speaks well and is enthusiastic.
>
> However there is one in particular (for French) who is atrocious. He does not use any audio-visuals. When you go online there is no PowerPoint, just a recording of him speaking … I am doing a whole unit on Dante with this dud lecturer. He sits down in the tutorial and looks bored for three hours. Young students are too scared to complain, but another mature age student and I both agreed we needed to say something. He has been teaching for 25 years and I thought about all those poor students.

Student E, an Art teacher in Egypt, had a different slant on what makes a good teacher. She spoke more about her own teaching experience in Egypt rather than her Australian teachers of her Certificate 1V course.

> When I was an Art teacher it was like a big family. I had lots of students that other teachers found difficult, but they were no trouble in my class.
>
> I can't think of any unhelpful lecturers. But I am a visual learner. That is how I learn, but I also find writing down notes helps.

Of course, different adult students learn in different ways. The principles of Universal Design for Learning take account of this, without falling into the trap of assigning learners to categories. Generally speaking, providing more paths to learning, by providing information in different formats, helps everybody learn better. So, as well as tutors taking the time to get to know their adult learners, UDL can help take account of cultural diversity as well as individual strengths, preferences and challenges.

## Supporting adult learners returning to study

We have already touched on the importance of you as an adult educator recognising your role as official sources of support for returning adult learners. However, educator support is not the only support inclusive institutions must offer. Institutional-level support must also be effective.

## Conclusion

We know that adult learners are often highly motivated. Whether this motivation arises from extrinsic factors, such as the need to earn more money, or intrinsic factors such as the desire for self-improvement, you as a teacher, coach and mentor could capitalise on this motivation through creating inclusive learning environments: active, engaging and effective for all. To achieve this, you as an adult educator need to be mindful of both the challenges learners from diverse cultural backgrounds face, and the principles of what makes a good educator.

## Provocation

Checklist for including learners from diverse cultural backgrounds

| Cultural aspects of inclusive education | Yes | No | Review |
|---|---|---|---|
| Do you know what your adult learner's motivation is for being on your course? | | | |
| Have you taken the time to discover the cultural diversity you have in your group? | | | |
| Are you aware of the obstacles your adult learners face that might make study difficult for them? | | | |
| Do you have a process to enable relevant teaching staff to access this information so they may be better informed, particularly about the needs and issues of refugee adult learners? | | | |
| Have you considered how you can use the cultural and 'life experience' riches to enhance the learning outcomes of the group? | | | |
| Have you investigated the support mechanisms that are available for the needs of your group, both internally in your organisation and externally but available to your adult learners? | | | |
| Do you modify your teaching practices to account for cultural diversity? | | | |
| Is your curriculum and teaching materials accessible and appropriate for all? | | | |
| What is the first thing you could do to make yourself a better educator of adults? | | | |

## References

Armstrong, C., Armstrong, D. and Spandagou, I. (2010). *Inclusive education: International policy and practice*. London: SAGE.

Bouchard, P. (2006). Human capital and the knowledge eEconomy. In: T. Fenwick, T. Nesbit, and B. Spencer, (eds), *Contexts of adult education: Canadian perpsectives*. Toronto: Thompson Educational Publishing.

Bowl, M. (2001). Experiencing the barriers: Non-traditional students entering higher education. *Research Papers in Education*, 16 (2), 141–160. DOI: 10.1080/02671520110037410

CAST (2012). What is UDL? [online] http://www.udlcenter.org/aboutudl/whatisudl [accessed 15 June 2015].

Centre for Multicultural Youth (CMY), Melbourne (2015). YouTube videos. *Tips for Tutors* http://cmy.net.au/standard/video-resources

Coffield, F., Moseley, D., Hall, E. and Ecclestone, K. (2004). *Should we be using learning styles? What research has to say to practice*. London: Learning and Skills Research Centre.

Frumkin, L. A. and Koutsoubou, M. (2013). Exploratory investigation of drivers of attainment in ethnic minority adult learners, *Journal of Further and Higher Education*, 37(2), 147–162. DOI: 10.1080/0309877X.2011.644777

Hart, S., Dixon, A., Drummond, M. J. and McIntyre, D. (2004). *Learning without limits*. Maidenhead: Open University Press

Hodkinson, A. and Vickerman, P. (2009). *Key issues in special educational needs and inclusion*. London: SAGE.

Hyland, T. and Merrill, B. (2003). *The changing face of further education: Lifelong learning, inclusion and community values in further education*. London: Routledge.

Knowles, M. (1980). *The modern practice of adult education*. New York: Cambridge Adult Education Company.

LSDA (Learning and Skills Development Agency) (2004). Disability Discrimination Act: Taking the work forward. *Research and development projects 2003/5. Project 9 Specific Cultural Requirements of Learners From Ethnic Minority Groups*. London: LSDA.

United Nations High Commission for Refugees. (2002). *The refugee resettlement handbook*. Geneva Switzerland: UNHCR. http://www.unhcr.org

Victorian Foundation for Survivors of Torture Inc. (VFST) (2011). *School's in for refugees; A whole-school approach to supporting students of refugee background*. (2nd Ed). Available here: http://www.foundationhouse.org.au/schools-refugees-2nd-edition-2011/

Chapter 6

# Education provision for sight impaired adult learners

*Celia McDonald and Susan Rodrigues*

## Introduction

Providing adult learners with professional development is challenging. Being aware of some of the challenges that may arise when working with adults is key to you being an effective and reflective educator. In previous chapters in this book various adult learning theories and principles are described with a view to illustrating how to develop programmes that could provide adult learners with an effective and encouraging learning experience. In this case study we reflect on how to best supervise, mentor, coach, and teach adult learners who have a visual impairment. In this chapter we are using the Ponchillia and Ponchillia (1996) view of visual impairment – any degree of vision loss, including total blindness that affects an individual's ability to perform the tasks of daily life. This may include some of the following: low vision, blindness, congenitally blind, adventitiously blind and blind with light perception only (unable to distinguish shape, but aware of presence of light – sometimes with direction/source of light, sometimes not).

Ponchillia and Ponchillia (1996) labelled a degree of vision that is functional but limited to the point of interference as low vision. In these cases people with low vision have impairments that cannot be corrected through the use of standard eyeglasses or contact lenses. Ponchillia and Ponchillia (1996) labelled the lack of functional vision as blindness. Lowenfeld (1973) wrote that it was generally accepted that children younger than five years old who lost their sight tended not to retain useful visual imagery or the notion of colour. Those who lost their vision before age five are referred to as congenitally blind (Lowenfeld, 1973). Those whose vision becomes impaired after age five are referred to as adventitiously (occurring or appearing later in life) blind (Corn and Koenig, 1996). However, for some people with this condition they can discern the presence or absence of light but cannot identify the source or direction (Corn and Koenig, 1996). Given this array of visual impairments, each eye condition has functional implications. Consequently the impact of any visual impairment on any specific learner is unique to that learner.

## Learning environments

As a consequence of the current economic climate it has become increasingly difficult to access and receive financial or care assistance. As a result many visually impaired adults are seeking professional development to improve their employment prospects, increase their independence, and/or maintain their self-respect and dignity. Many visually impaired adults are seeking this professional development in a variety of subjects, from specialists and mainstream provision. While specialists may be familiar with the challenges and rewards faced when supporting visually impaired adults in their learning endeavours, for some in mainstream provision, the challenges and rewards are new and possibly daunting.

Visually impaired adults, like most adults 'tend to be goal and relevancy-oriented, learn experientially, and approach learning as problem-solving' (Sherman et al., 2000, p. 4). However, as Schwier (1995) wrote, 'We must allow circumstances surrounding the learning situation to help us decide which approach to learning is most appropriate. It is necessary to realise that some learning problems require highly prescriptive solutions, whereas others are more suited to learner control of the environment' (p. 119).

Adult learning theories include Brookfield's theory of adult learning, Daloz's theory of adult learning, Kolb's theory of experiential learning (1984), and Schön's (1983, 1987) theory of reflection on learning (see Chapter 3 in this book). Brookfield's (1983) theory advocates that a learner sets the direction for the learning and learning needs to be relevant. Schön (1983, 1987), Kolb (1984) and Mezirow (1991) all signal the importance of prior experience and suggest that experiences can be put to use as a resource for learning. Daloz (1986) identifies the importance of a readiness to learn, and suggests that mature learning becomes orientated towards tasks associated with the development of social roles. Kolb (1984) identifies the need for transformative experience to support an orientation to learning. While Maslow (1970) and Locke (1968, 1996) suggest a motivation to learn develops with maturity. As a result as seen in Chapter 5 in this book, there is a focus on connecting a sense of purpose with a goal or identification of a result. Sherman et al. (2000) draw on the literature to argue that a constructivist approach enables adult learners to learn best. Adult learning is most effective when adult learners:

- establish links between new and prior experiences;
- use prior experiences during the learning process;
- contribute to the planning of their learning;
- have learning options;
- have opportunities to analyse and develop what they learn;
- have opportunities to apply what they learn in a personal practical milieu.

In this chapter we try to show how you as an adult educator can use a constructivist approach with adult learners with a visual impairment. We begin by considering some of the misconceptions that exist with regard to coaching, mentoring, supervising and generally educating visually impaired adults. We consider some of the strategies that you could use to better support visually impaired adults seeking education and we identify an assessment protocol that could be used to establish aims and the objectives to achieve specific goals.

## Misconceptions

There are several common misconceptions that are held by visually impaired people themselves, or their families and friends, and/or the public in general. A few of the common misconceptions are described below.

Misconception 1: *When people lose their sight their hearing and other senses improve to compensate for the loss.*

This may not actually be the case. The reality is that people with a visual impairment may rely more heavily on their other senses and so pay more attention to them than they did before. So while the other senses are not suddenly enhanced, visually impaired people's awareness of the contribution of their other senses grows.

Misconception 2: *If someone has a white cane, or guide dog, s/he must be blind and blind means totally blind.*

To be registered as blind, means that the level of vision is lower than someone who is registered as partially sighted. Blind does not mean totally blind. Less than 4% of registered blind people are totally blind. As a rehabilitation officer, Celia often receives telephone calls from the public to report someone who 'must have stolen a guide dog' or 'white stick', because s/he boarded a bus with one and then started reading a newspaper! That person may be partially sighted or even 'blind' and have good acuity but a very limited field of vision (tunnel vision). Hence the person can read print, but not see the bollard directly in front, or notice the person to the side of her or himself trying to get her/his attention by waving, because it is not within the blind person's field of vision. White canes and dogs are mobility aids and/or a form of identification (in contrast to a wheelchair user, a visual impairment is not necessarily an obvious or visible disability).

Misconception 3: *All blind people can read Braille.*

As stated earlier, most blind people have some residual vision and therefore may be able to read standard print because they have lost their field of vision, not acuity. Or they may be able to read large print in certain colours with particular lighting. Plus some eye conditions come with other health problems. For instance diabetic retinopathy is as a result of diabetes which can also cause peripheral neuropathy, so making reading Braille almost impossible. However the main reason people choose not to read Braille in the present day is due to the abundance of technology available to assist them with communication. Mobile phones or computers have the ability to scan, speak, enlarge or change font, colour and lighting and are readily available, versatile, affordable and compatible with various social networks (Internet, email, etc.). There are also more specialist items of technology that negate the need for learning to read Braille, which can be bulky, time consuming and flatten easily.

Misconception 4: *It is better to be born blind than to go blind later in life.*

While there is the school of thought that you do not miss what you have never had, this statement is neither right nor wrong. While some theorists compare losing your sight to bereavement, the advantage of being 'adventitiously blind', rather than 'congenitally blind', is the acquired visual knowledge. Hence, if someone had sight before, s/he would have a better understanding of colour or distance, and have prior visual knowledge of her/his environment and objects. However, it would mean that s/he would have to learn to do most things in a different way. Whereas someone who is 'congenitally blind', would not have to deal with the same emotional trauma, or learn to do things in a different way.

Misconception 5: *A guide dog is a better mobility aid than a long cane.*

A guide dog can be a much more sociable mobility aid than a long cane. It appears that in general, the public have a positive attitude to guide dog users, engaging in conversation about the dog. However, long cane users tend to be pitied and so ignored or avoided. However, a guide dog will guide her/his owner around an object, so the owner is less aware of the environment than a long cane user. This point was demonstrated when Celia had to train a guide dog user how to use a long cane to get to work. When teaching the route Celia identified several permanent landmarks along the way (lamp posts, post box, shrubbery) – none of which the person had been aware of before. Plus the person commented that while the public were not as friendly, he did not have to worry about cleaning up after it, feeding it or entertaining it – he just threw the cane in the cupboard.

## Strategies and considerations

Sight loss can be a barrier to learning. It is a barrier to learning not just in terms of the information being inaccessible. It is also a barrier to learning as a consequence of other distractions and obstacles that need to be overcome either before, or during, the course of a tutoring/coaching/mentoring session. As an adult educator you need to ensure that these distractions and obstacles are identified within the initial assessment/meeting and constantly monitored so that they are being addressed appropriately and adequately.

It is very common for people whose sight has deteriorated to say that their memory is worse now, because they keep forgetting where they put things or what they were about to do. The loss of visual prompts (an important part of the memory process) can contribute towards someone thinking they are forgetful. Hence the modelling form of teaching (hands on) may sometimes be beneficial as a memory aid when there are no visual cues. Bear in mind that trying to remember all of the information just aurally without visual cues is a major task. Hence with sight loss the use of vocabulary takes on an added significance.

This includes communicating what is being done, or reading/describing any displays (diagrammatic or written). It is always worthwhile discussing with the adult learner in advance alternative ways of presenting information. However, for the sake of dignity and privacy avoid having these discussions/assessments in front of a group.

Therefore, you as an adult educator must consider chunking, recapping and reviewing progress as a necessity. This will help to ensure that the adult learner has absorbed and understood what is being taught before moving onto the next stage. It is also worth considering that achieving the objective by the end of a session can often be the reward in itself and thereby increase self-esteem, motivation and focus. Therefore extra time may be needed in order for a visually impaired adult learner to read through information, assimilate the information and respond before going to the next stage. Bear in mind that it is not possible to skim read when reading Braille, which can take up to three times as long as other learners reading text, or if the person has a special computer with the translated text available.

Listening is just as essential in reviewing as it is when assessing. Otherwise preconceptions from past experiences, may lead to hearing what one expects to hear. As Stanton (1996) wrote, 'The only listening that counts is that of the talker who alternately absorbs and expresses ideas' (p. 24). For example, consider the following scenario: During the assessment a history educator in adult education listened to the adult learner state how much she enjoyed typing before and would like to do the course via a computer. After investigation the history educator sourced software that he felt was suitable for the adult learner's needs. However, as the lessons progressed the adult learner found that she was struggling with the software. But the educator just reassured her that she would get used to it, as it was the most suitable software for blind people. However, this did not prove to be the case. The adult learner was about to give up the course, but approached Celia (as her rehabilitation officer) about this problem. Upon further discussion Celia explained that because the adult learner lost her sight later in life she was not accustomed to listening to speech at such a high speed. So adjusting the speed may help reduce this problem. Also the adult learner's hearing loss was never identified at the assessment stage and the fact that she wore a hearing aid had never been noticed. Hence the educator did not realise that the adult learner was hard of hearing. In this scenario, headphones were sufficient, but if not Celia would have given the educator a contact for specialist advice regarding technology for the hard of hearing. Plus while the adult learner enjoyed typing she was not familiar with the terminology used with this particular software. So although the software was suitable for blind people the adult learner needed to be taught how to use the technology, before starting the course. While reviewing was a step in the right direction by the educator he had failed to listen, observe and act upon what the adult learner was experiencing.

Preparation is an essential part of teaching. While lack of preparation can reduce the effectiveness of teaching sighted people, it would be far more detrimental to visually impaired people. A visually impaired person may automatically assume the difficulty is due to her/his sight loss. This may result in reducing her/his self-esteem and having a negative influence on her/his working relationship with the teacher. When working with a visually impaired person, preparation should include what was identified in the assessment, as well as the availability of resources and who is responsible for providing particular materials (Braille, large print, support worker, specialist computer). For example, if the assessment identified a particular lighting requirement, this would need to be addressed within the preparation (any requirement for specific task lighting, blinds, particular settings on a computer, etc.). If large print is required what font size and what colours are best suited for the adult learner (black font size 14 on a yellow background is a good start, as most find white provides too much glare. But individuals have different requirements). Sans serif fonts (such as Arial) are usually the better font styles in sentence case (not capitals) and never on glossy paper. Reading lists, or course outlines, should be given to visually impaired adult learners well in advance to allow time for making it accessibly formatted (Braille transcription, recording, etc). If the reading list is long, identify which texts are a priority if possible. If these sorts of things are not assessed and identified at an early stage, at best it will be a very slow and frustrating progress and at worst the adult learner will give up and leave with less confidence and self-worth than s/he arrived with.

The environment in which visually impaired people learn is a crucial part of the learning process. Too much background noise makes it difficult for visually impaired people to communicate. They do not have the advantage of lip reading, or reading print or interpreting a visual cue. Thus background noise can be a distraction. Furthermore, moving furniture or resources around can be very disorientating and therefore distracting from the actual learning process. As Buckley and Caple (1991) suggested, the learning environment needs to maintain an adult learner's alertness throughout.

However, it is also worth stating that sight loss often accompanies other diminishing capacities and capabilities. For example, most people's sight deteriorates with age. Unfortunately so do other things as well – hearing, mobility, or general health. Many people acquire sight loss as a result of other health conditions such as diabetes, brain injuries (including strokes), heart attacks, etc. These health conditions also impact upon the individual in other ways. For example, there may be a reduction in her/his peripheral and autonomic neuropathy, cognition or memory. Therefore, as indicated in the section on misconceptions, while the other senses may not compensate for sight loss, you as a well-prepared adult educator will have assessed the limitations, or preferences of your visually impaired adult learner.

When teaching, supervising, coaching or mentoring a visually impaired person it is crucial that the visually impaired person has been assessed properly. This will help establish her/his eye condition, and provide background information, for example on how long s/he has had it and its affects, as this may also have an impact on her/his ability and capability in a new learning environment. Someone who has recently become visually impaired may not have developed an array of strategies to help her/himself. In contrast someone who has been long-term visually impaired may be more able to draw on a suitable array of strategies to help her/himself in a new learning environment. Similarly, some eye conditions vary in affect depending upon how far it has progressed. For instance diabetes has many physical complications and diabetic retinopathy can have varying consequences on vision. The condition may occur with male or female, young and old people. Hence the needs of people with diabetic retinopathy vary drastically. Glaucoma sometimes affects peripheral vision, or the opposite central vision, or all vision. It sometimes affects night vision and can cause severe glare problems during the day and/or night. If you conduct an assessment it could establish what lighting conditions best suit that particular person to enhance her/his ability to function/learn. For example, the adult learner could be seated with the window directly behind them, or need a task lamp directly over their work, or need to be in the corner away from the window, or need to wear sunglasses to improve what vision they do have.

Some visually impaired adult learners have stopped attending classes because of the 'innocent' ridicule received for wearing sunglasses indoors; some have even been instructed to remove them if they wanted to attend the class. All these avoidable 'small' obstacles can be very discouraging for visually impaired people, who may still be coming to terms with their sight loss and who do not want to draw attention to themselves or their disability. 'Coping with sight loss has to take place on the perceptual, the behavioural, the cognitive and the emotional levels' (Dodds, 1993, p. 33).

As stated previously in this chapter, the use of vocabulary is extremely important when working with visually impaired people. Common mistakes, for example just saying it is 'over there' or using descriptors to describe visual similarities (congenitally blind) like 'fluffy as a cloud' or 'a golden yellow' are not very useful or productive. Or if text is being referred to for example, rather than stating 'follow the instructions in paragraph three', it is probably better to read out paragraph three. If the visually impaired person has an audio recording of the information, it would be near impossible to find paragraph three, or, as stated earlier, a Braille reader would take much longer to find paragraph three.

Again the use of vocabulary depends upon the individual's knowledge and vision. The person's understanding of left and right may not be reliable. Instead using the environment as a cue can help, albeit depending on the sight and hearing level. For example, instructions such as 'towards the brighter side' or 'in the direction of the noisy corridor' may work as better directors for some visually impaired adult learners. Again this demonstrates the importance of an assessment at the outset to establish the extent of adult learners' useful vision and hearing, at what stage in life their sight began to deteriorate, their level of knowledge and perception of their environment.

Communication is a means of transferring and transforming information. In some cases body language forms an important part of communication. However, visually impaired people cannot always decipher body language. As a result a lot more attention is placed on not only the language used, but also the tone of voice used to communicate the information. Tone has a significant role to play in establishing a relationship between a visually impaired person and the adult educator. Consequently, communication influences not only the relationship with the adult learner but also the efficiency of the teaching process. It is essential that you as an adult educator always identify yourself when addressing a visually impaired student. Associated with the misconception of improved hearing is the misconception that a visually impaired person can easily recognise a voice. This is much easier when accompanied by visual identification.

We have established that a thorough assessment and preparation is vital. While most information can be obtained from the adult learner, further information can be obtained from other sources. If the adult learner is agreeable s/he could show you his/her Certificate of Visual Impairment (CVI) from the hospital. The CVI would identify the eye condition, level of acuity and field of vision in each eye. It will also state whether a magnifying or lighting assessment will be carried out and it will supply the address of the department that deals with such assessments and rehabilitation. The CVI would also tell you if there were any other notable health conditions such as hearing loss (do they wear a hearing aid? Would a loop system help?) mobility (is the location physically accessible?) and memory or dexterity problems (would a reading volunteer/support worker be useful?).

The department dealing with the assessments and rehabilitation would be able to give you advice, information and other avenues about the adult learner's abilities, requirements (i.e. lighting, font size, colour, etc.), eye condition and the implications of these. In the United Kingdom the RNIB is the national visual impairment organisation. The RNIB would be able to provide general advice and literature about different eye conditions, resources available in different parts of the country and contact details – particularly useful if a CVI is unobtainable (for further information visit www.rnib.org.uk). Other countries have an equivalent organisation, for example, Australia has Vision Australia (for further information visit www.visionaustralia.org).

An individual assessment at the beginning of any adult education programme or professional development would enable you as the adult educator to reduce possible obstacles.

## Assessment to establish aims and the objectives to reach those goals

The purpose of an assessment is to mutually establish the adult learner's aims, and the necessary objectives to achieve those aims. A good assessment should:

- promote participation and establish a trusting relationship, through good communication;

- not only assess the needs, but identify strengths, weaknesses and available resources;
- agree realistic objectives with the visually impaired person – including specific outcomes and mutual responsibilities.

For example a naval chef who was forced to take early retirement due to his sight loss, wanted to be able to cook again but had very little useful sight. Using his experience and expertise it was agreed what recipe would involve the largest variety of skills needed. His existing kitchen environment was then addressed – organising the shelves so that everything was in a logical place for him and therefore more easily remembered. A lighting assessment was carried out to ensure the kitchen lighting made the best use of his useful vision, as did the layout of the worktop. The next stage was how he would control and operate appliances (tactile marking up in some instances while others just needed a clock face analogy). This constituted part of the assessment as well as teaching (but all in collaboration with the adult learner), before even beginning on how to prepare a certain dish.

The assessment process can be divided into three parts:

- *Opening*: Introduce yourself, your organisation and the purpose of the assessment. A clear platform is established from which the assessment can proceed.
- *Body*: Establish the adult learner's present capabilities, his/her needs and prioritising those needs. There are different recognised models of assessment such as the questioning, exchange or procedural models. The exchange model of assessment is not just a process of asking a list of questions, it is observing the adult learner's behaviour, listening to what s/he says (not just in response to the questions), and discussing with the adult learner what her/his strengths are, what s/he find difficult and why, and past experiences (good and bad). The exchange model increases the learner's trust and acknowledges her/his strengths as it encourages the learner to feel valued because her/his expertise is being recognised. '... It is dangerous to overlook multiple identities and to assume that disability is the sole significant identity' (French et al., 1997, p. 6). This enforces the Corn and Koenig (1996) model, that there are three types of factors that influence the process of learning. Hence a holistic approach is required whereby all the following must be considered:
    - Visual abilities – acuity, visual field, eye movement, brain function and light and colour perception.
    - Environmental cues – colour (saturation, brightness, and hue), contrast (intensity, tone, and colour), space (outline, size, complexity, pattern and clutter), illumination (distance, reflectance, and intensity).
    - Stored and available individuality – physical and psychological makeup (general health, emotional stability, motivation, attention and identity as a sighted, partially sighted or blind person), cognition, past experiences and ability to use other senses to make sense of visual information and perceptions.

- *Closing*: The assessment must end at some point. For some adult learners if the assessment has been an interactive process it may have been the first time someone has actually listened to their opinions and so may not want this stage to finish. If you focus on what was achieved in that session and what will happen in the next, it could promote the adult learners' self-esteem. Since an assessment is a mutual exchange of information, adult learners should be involved throughout.

Returning to the naval chef; in this instance the adult learner had visual memories that were of benefit to him, however being visually impaired was new to him so he had to learn to do things all over again in a different way. Hence preparing the dish was further broken down into manageable portions (chunking) – how to measure different types of ingredients, preparing ingredients (cutting, peeling, etc.), mixing to required consistency and finally cooking – knowing when to stop, turn over, mix or adjust temperature. Initially the entire process was run through, so that the adult learner was aware of the plan. The chunking process was explained to the adult learner so that he was aware of what was expected of him at each lesson and what the desired outcome was before moving onto the next stage. Chunking allows for reflecting upon the task learned or practised, making sense of it and accordingly adapting the next lesson. Plus it enables recapping which is important to facilitate retention of knowledge, skills and the appropriateness of methods used. This method accommodates the fact that unless someone is totally blind, her/his sight may fluctuate on a daily, weekly or more irregular basis. Consequently what s/he may be able to see or identify one day, s/he may not the next day, making constant monitoring and re-evaluation imperative.

## Conclusion

Most visually impaired people start to lose their sight in adulthood. Unfortunately people tend to forget when meeting someone with a visual impairment that some have some knowledge and experience from before they lost their sight and after. Losing your sight does not mean you have lost your mental capacity. Consequently acknowledging the adult learner's knowledge, understanding and expertise not only improves the teaching relationship but aids the teaching process. Hopefully this chapter has demonstrated to you that all aspects discussed are interdependent and form part of a learning cycle, not just a linear order of events. Therefore, regardless of the amount of information available, one's own experience, or how often one has met the adult learner, there is a constant need to evaluate oneself, the information and the adult learner. This is a unique and dynamic process – which is generally good practice when educating regardless of sight loss. However assessment and preparation is vital when working with someone with a visual impairment.

## Provocation

The JKLMNO approach outlined below can be used as a checklist to ascertain the needs of an adult learner (and not necessarily only adult learners with a visual impairment) who you may be working with in the future.

**Justification**: The learner and the tutor/coach/mentor/supervisor need to have had a conversation to justify what is to be done, what sort of commitment is sought, and the boundaries.

**Know**: What is it that is being sought? Examine the task and determine what exactly is being sought in terms of component tasks.

**Learning**: What is the specification? Identify the task and determine what further information is required to ensure potential tutoring/mentoring/coaching bridges the gap.

**Match**: Give some thought to matching strategies to the character of the learner (age, impairment, experience).

**Needs**: This should identify a gap which forms the basis for the tutoring/mentoring/supervising in terms of what experience is needed to understand (use to know) and what guidance may be useful to understand (useful to know). Negotiate the content.

**Objectives**: Write down unambiguously exactly what the learners are expected to be able to do/know as a result of her/his learning experience. This can include the performance expected in terms of knowledge and skills. It can include the conditions that define the context in which the knowledge and skills are carried out. It can include the standard or level of performance to be achieved.

## References

Brookfield, S. (1983). *Adult learning, adult education and the community.* Milton Keynes: Open University Press.

Buckley, R. and Caple, J. (1991). *The theory and practice of training.* London: Kogan Page.

Corn, A. L. and Koenig, A. J. (1996). *Foundation of low vision: Clinical and functional perspectives (Foundation Series).* New York: American Foundation for the Blind.

Daloz, L. A. (1986). *Effective teaching and mentoring: Realizing the transformational power of adult learning experiences.* San Francisco, CA: Jossey-Bass.

Dodds, A. (1993). *Rehabilitating blind and visually impaired people: A psychological approach.* Dodrecht: Springer+ Business Media.

French, S., Gillman, M. and Swain, J. (1997). *Working with visually disabled people: bridging theory and practice.* Birmingham: Venture Press.

Kolb, D. A. (1984). *Experiential learning.* Englewood Cliffs, NJ: Prentice Hall.

Locke, E. A. (1968). Toward a theory of task motivation and incentives. *Organizational Behavior and Human Performance*, 3, 157–189.

Locke, E. A. (1996). Motivation through conscious goal setting. *Applied & Preventive Psychology*, 5, 117–124.

Lowenfeld, B. (1973). *The visually handicapped child in school.* New York: The John Day Company.

Maslow, A. H. (1970). *Motivation and personality.* New York: Harper and Row.

Mezirow, J. (1991). *Transformative dimensions in adult learning.* San Francisco: Jossey-Bass.

Ponchillia, P. E. and Ponchillia, S. V. (1996). *Foundation of rehabilitation teaching with persons who are blind or visually impaired.* New York: American Foundation for the Blind.

Schön, D. A. (1983). *The reflective practitioner: How professionals think in action.* London: Maurice Temple Smith.

Schön, D. A. (1987). *Educating the reflective practitioner: Toward a new design for teaching and learning in the professions.* San Francisco, CA: Jossey-Bass.

Schwier, R. A. (1995). Issues in emerging interactive technologies. In G. J. Anglin, (Ed.) *Instructional technology: Past, present and future.* (2nd edn). Englewood, CO: Libraries Unlimited.

Sherman, R., Voight, J., Tibbetts, J., Dobbins, D., Evans, A., Weidler, D. and the Pelavin Research Institute. (2000). *Adult educators' guide to designing instructor mentoring.* Retrieved from http://www.calpro-online.org/pubs/Mentoring%20 Guide.pdf Accessed 16 May 2016.

Stanton, N. (1996). *Mastering communication.* London: McMillan/Open University.

Chapter 7

# The use of technology in the supervision and teaching of medical education

*Susie Schofield, Madawa Chandratilake and Hiroshi Nishigori*

## Medical education

In the preface to *Problem-based learning: An approach to medical education*, Robyn Tamblyn encapsulates medical education as: 'the need to actively apply knowledge to the assessment and care of patients and the ability to continue to identify areas where further learning would enhance or improve the practice of these skills' (Tamblyn, 1980, p. xiii). The cost of educating medical students is not insignificant. In 2012 a national newspaper in the UK reported that it cost the tax payer £250,000 to put one student through the five years of the undergraduate medical school (Smith, 2012), and of course the cost to patient health, if badly done, goes beyond money.

In order to inform your use of technology as an adult educator this chapter looks specifically at how technology is currently used by adult educators in the teaching and supervision of medical students and trainees. The chapter highlights areas of interest in three settings: UK, Sri Lanka and Japan. Each setting has a different training structure, culture and level of technology immersion of its adult learners, teachers, health practitioners and patients. Each of these has implications for how technology is used and how it might be further exploited by adult educators in a way acceptable to relevant stakeholders.

Throughout this chapter, we present thinking points that you as an adult educator could apply within your own context for each section, and encourage you to discuss these with your colleagues, mentees and trainees.

## Qualifying as a doctor in the UK, Sri Lanka and Japan

There are 33 undergraduate medical schools offering the MBChB / MBBS in the UK. The degree is usually five years in duration with the option of an extra intercalated year. The newly-qualified Foundation Year doctors (FYs) then join the two-year Foundation Programme whose curriculum is set out and regulated by the General Medical Council (GMC) (General Medical Council, 2015) to standardise medical training across the UK, followed by specialty training.

In Sri Lanka, eight medical schools, all faculties of state-owned universities, offer the MBBS degree then a one-year internship. Admission to medical schools is centralised and solely based on students' academic performance, and programmes are largely uniform except for elective components. A national curriculum for competencies in undergraduate medical education is available for benchmarking. Unlike in the UK, postgraduate medical education is delivered by a single institution, with length depending on the discipline. Graduates should complete a minimum of one year foreign training before being board certified as consultants.

Japan has 79 medical schools, and the programme is six years long, again with the majority of students coming straight from school. A nationwide common achievement test which students must pass to qualify for pre-clinical medical education was introduced in 2005. Postgraduates must train for a further two years before specialising (Kozu, 2006).

## Use of technology

The use of technology in teaching and supervision falls into three areas: technology-enhanced learning, learning about the technology used in the workplace, and professionalism issues relating to technology. Each has seen massive changes in the last 20 years, driven by the increasing power and decreasing cost of computers, development of the web, increased coverage of Wi-Fi, and use of mobile devices (Baker and Evans, 2011).

## The medical lecture

UK undergraduate medical schools now use virtual learning environments (VLE) to support their students. These adult students expect lecture notes to be put up on the VLE before a lecture so they can pre-read and either print out or, increasingly, download onto their mobile device, annotating as the lecture takes place or just sitting and listening. Although print costs now fall on the individual student rather than the institution, tutors have expressed concerns about a) decreasing attendance b) students not paying attention if they are not busy writing notes and c) using their devices for other unrelated purposes. Most research in this area suggests attendance has not decreased and that student attainment has improved (Karnad, 2013).

The medical lecture itself has transformed with the use of technology. PowerPoint has replaced the whiteboard in most lectures, though some are now using Prezi as a tool more suited to teaching where the subject matter benefits from zooming in on detail (Tam and Eastwood, 2012). In medical education, you as an adult educator may have to use Webcams and visualisers as they can project images of items where in the past they were handed round the class, or they can be used outside the lecture hall, e.g. in theatre, to project back to the lecture (Russomano et al., 2009).

YouTube is widely used both in the lecture hall and online (Jaffar, 2012). In some fields such as pharmacology, the construction of concept maps by the tutor has proved a more effective learning tool than merely portraying the finished article on a PowerPoint (Daley and Torre, 2010). In the latter years of undergraduate training and beyond, students are often geographically displaced, and can join live lectures via webinars or watch the recording after the event (Alnabelsi et al., 2015). In medical education, lectures can be followed by online tasks/learning, or in some cases the lecture may only be part of an online experience. There has also been increasing interest in the flipped classroom where students review lectures online and the traditional face-to-face (F2F) lecture time is used for more active learning, e.g. a tutorial or a questions and answers session (McLaughlin et al., 2014). As an adult educator you may wish to take on board Prober and Khan's (2013) advice to give students prior access to online videos on new concepts to view in their own time, as many times as they wish prior to a F2F interactive session applying this newly mastered knowledge.

In Sri Lanka, basic technology like PowerPoint has been in common use across undergraduate and postgraduate education. Free learning management systems (LMS) such as Moodle (open-source, hence free) have been increasingly used in medical schools. As a developing country that offers medical education free of charge, commercially available systems are unaffordable. Development costs are kept to a minimum by collaborative efforts between medical and IT faculties. Students in the IT faculties undertake projects in developing multi-media learning objects for the LMSs. This is mutually beneficial as the projects provide work-based assessment opportunities for IT students and interactive computer-based learning material for medical students.

In Japan, as some teaching hospitals and clinics are located in remote areas, supervisors who are in charge of the postgraduate training programme are actively using videoconference systems, like Skype and WebEx, which is cheap and easy to use. International meetings are also increasingly being held via webinars, reducing travel costs, both in terms of time and money. Availability of video archives of seminars from academic conferences e.g. the Association for Medical Education in Europe (AMEE) AMEE Live's *Ming Jung Ho symposium* (AMEE, 2014) is a useful addition to CPD (Continuing Professional Development). The majority of the seminars and lectures in the Japanese Society of Internal Medicine (JSIM) annual conferences are video-recorded every year, so that members of the JSIM can view them afterwards (JSIM, 2015a). In 2015, the JSIM introduced a web-based CPD (self-assessment) tool for its members as part of assessment for board re-certification (JSIM, 2015b). The University of Tokyo and Kyoto University, the so called 'Oxbridge' of Japan, have both created platforms of open course ware (OCW). Anyone who is interested can see selected seminars and lectures in this OCW site. Although most content is in Japanese, some are in English. The aims of the OCW in many medical schools and universities are a) to share 'knowledge' of the universities to the public, and b) to recruit students. The number of the seminars available, although small at present, has been increasing.

**Thinking point:** Your mentee has been asked to present a lecture to third year undergraduates on professionalism in the workplace. She is confident with the content, but worries about making the material relevant and engaging. Consider each of these options in your own context:

- use of video, e.g. YouTube showing lapses in professional behaviour;
- audience response system to survey opinion on severity of lapses and sanctions;
- use of flipped classroom model to set pre-reading and online discussion.

What other technology-enhanced approaches can you suggest?

## The clinical setting

The clinical setting is a powerful context for learning, where teaching can occur formally during ward rounds and ward-based tutorials, or informally as an apprentice. There is an increasing interest in the use of mobile technology on the ward (Davies et al., 2012), where some clinicians already use it to access patient and other information (Kendall and Enright, 2012).

The importance of on-the-job role modelling and its enormous influence on learning has been well documented. Use of technology here can relate to using technology to complete a job, and using technology to learn about the job. Artefacts such as the British National Formulary (BNF) are now available online. Young doctors seem to be becoming more comfortable using mobile technology in front of their seniors and patients (Bullock et al., 2015). This may be due to role modelling by those more senior physicians (Koehler et al., 2013). Interestingly, research has shown patients of lower socio-economic standing are least accepting of doctors 'looking things up' on the web, though this may change with the increasing ubiquity of mobiles across the UK.

**Thinking point:** How is technology used in your equivalent clinical context, both as part of the job (e.g. hospital systems holding patient records) and as additional aids (e.g. BNF)? How do you reduce any potentially negative impact on the clinician / patient relationship of using technology during a consultation? Is this something you discuss and role model consciously with your adult trainees?

## The laboratory

QR (quick response) codes are being used increasingly within the laboratory setting, e.g. giving answers to posed questions tagged on cadaveric specimens

(Traser et al., 2015). The QR code can link to a textual answer, or hyperlinks, allowing potential use to show videos to individual students. Traser's team found reluctance from students to take their smartphones into the anatomy lab, showing the additional challenges medical educators face when patients and cadavers are present in the teaching environment.

## Simulation

Another area where technology is utilised in clinical teaching is in simulation, e.g. in procedural skills such as minimally invasive and open surgery, and endoscopy (Cook et al., 2013). As an adult educator in the medical education field you may have to use simulation technologies. Simulation technologies available in today's context are diverse and include computer-based virtual reality simulators, high-fidelity and static mannequins, plastic models, live animals, inert animal products, and human cadavers (Cook et al., 2011). The evidence suggests that technology-enhanced simulation training yields better educational outcome in relation to knowledge, skills, and behaviours and moderate effects for patient-related outcomes compared to no intervention. In Japan, Nara et al. (2009) found simulation-based learning to be uncommon due to a shortage of medical tutors, staff, mannequins and budget. In Sri Lanka simulation in many medical schools is low fidelity, restricted to a hybrid of simulated patients and models, primarily because of limited funds.

**Thinking point:** Deliberate practice refers to 'training activities that were most closely associated with consistent improvements in performance' (Ericsson, 2004, p. S72). In their review of the literature to 2010, McGaghie et al. (2011) found simulation-based medical education with deliberate practice more effective than traditional clinical medical education. As an adult educator, how do you ensure your adult trainees are able to spend time on deliberate practice on both technical and non-technical skills? Bearing in mind Chapter 3 on reflection and Chapter 4 on professional development, is reflection and professional development something you can maximise with the use of simulations?

## Telemedicine

Telemedicine offers huge potential to the health service, offering a cost-effective and time-efficient way to extend healthcare coverage to under-served areas e.g. rural areas and difficult areas such as prisons. It also provides access to specialists in general hospitals, and facilitates immediate evaluation. It may also reduce anxiety for registrars on night-shift worrying about calling their consultant in.

Because access to specialists (e.g. ophthalmologist or dermatologist) is sometimes difficult, we have seen an increasing number of telemedicine systems in Japan. For example, exMedio's Skin Disease Remote Diagnostic App (exMedio, 2015). Users (in many cases, general practitioners) download the app then enter the patient information with a picture of the skin involved. Board certified dermatologists send the differential diagnosis back to the users. At the time of writing this chapter, it was a free service.

> **Thinking point:** If you wish to deploy similar strategies to telemedicine, what are the training needs for those you supervise? How can it be harnessed to improve supervision? In light of the points made by McDonald and Rodrigues in Chapter 6 what would you need to put in place to support adults with sight impairments?

## Legalities and safe practice

In addition to guidance relating to copyright and online materials, e.g. that produced by JISC (2013), medical teachers in the UK are further guided by the GMC. For example, guidance on using visual and audio recordings relating to patients (General Medical Council, 2011) and confidentiality for education (General Medical Council, 2013). Online materials go beyond text, including graphics, videos, hyperlinks and audio. Increasingly they are developed for access on mobile as well as desk devices.

> **Thinking point:** Your trainee wants to use the equivalent (in your field) of patient data in her/his lecture and wants advice on the best way to proceed legally and ethically. What advice would you give him/her? What questions would you ask?

Another area increasingly of concern is that of adult learner and doctor use of social networking sites. Concerns have been raised about conflicts of interest and the patient/physician relationship (DeCamp, 2013), with McCartney (2012) questioning how much social online presence a physician can have. A recent lapse in professionalism involved doctors and nurses from the Great Western Hospital's Accident and Emergency Department and Acute Assessment Unit who photographed each other lying face down on resuscitation trolleys, ward floors and on the Wiltshire air ambulance helipad. These photographs were shared on a social media site where they came to the attention of a hospital manager, and the members of staff were suspended. Although they were all reinstated, the episode highlights the need for awareness of professionalism online (Australian Medical Council et al., 2010).

> **Thinking point**: Your mentee has asked to be your friend on a social networking site. What are the pros and cons to you as mentor and to your mentee?

## Facilitating learning

The shift from tutor to student-centred learning has seen the tutor role moving from dispenser of knowledge to facilitator of adult learning, creating self-directed lifelong adult learners. Many schools employ problem-based learning (PBL) to facilitate student-centred learning. Here a problem is presented to adult learners who, working in small groups, develop their own learning objectives in the first session, fulfil these individually, then reconvene to share and synthesise (Bligh, 1995). Traditionally adult learners have access to some resources during the F2F sessions, but not necessarily online. By combining PBL with web-based learning (WBL), Taradi and colleagues (Taradi et al., 2005) found adult learners on the hybrid mode were more motivated and satisfied, and performed better in the summative assessment. Another way technology can be used within PBL is by providing each PBL group with their own virtual space to use for discussions online between F2F sessions. This has been found to increase motivation levels and reduce misunderstandings, as the group tutor was able to correct these at an early stage of working (Alamro and Schofield, 2012). This study, along with many others, also found F2F shyer adult learners were more likely to participate online, and a rich range of multi-media resources were shared in the discussions. Online discussion boards have been set up with varying success to develop communities of learners among trainees.

## Using mobile devices for learning

One of the biggest shifts recently in technological advances in medical education is the use of mobile devices. Using computers to access online material went some way to move from teacher-centred to student-centred learning (Holzinger et al., 2005). The use of mobile devices for learning (m-learning) allows learners to access material virtually wherever and whenever they wish. Mobile devices such as mobile phones are widespread and commonly available even in resource-limited countries (The Asian Age, 2012). In North America, mobile device use among trainees and trainers is over 85% (Franko and Tirrell, 2012). Wallace et al. (2012) found evidence of use of these devices for educational and patient care purposes occurring in all settings where learners and teachers are present, from the classroom to the hospital. Learners use mobile devices mainly for information management (by accessing online textbooks, medical journal websites, medical podcasts, medical calculators, online lectures; taking notes; defining unfamiliar terms), communication (using email, telephone and text messages to communicate with peers, teachers and other members of the healthcare team about patient care), and time management (by accessing timetables and calendars 'on the go') (Davies et al., 2012). The mobile phone's portability, flexibility, access to multi-media and the ability to look up information quickly are all advantageous for education. The development of medical practice and medical education apps for mobile devices has substantially increased the use of these devices, especially smartphones. In the US, about 50% of medical trainers and trainees use smartphone apps in clinical practice mainly for educational purposes such as accessing general medical knowledge, treatment algorithms and drug guides (Franko and Tirrell, 2012). However, Davies et al. (2012) warn that learning through mobile devices may be superficial and users may not be aware of how to find good learning resources in mobile access. In a healthcare setting, where the educational component competes with service delivery, use of the mobile phone may be a distractor. Users may also be concerned about their privacy. However, although students, trainees and trainers in medicine use technology for educational purposes, they continue to consult with seniors and other members of the team (Bullock et al., 2015).

There are many examples of mobile device use in medical education in the literature, e.g. aiding problem-based learning as part of the formal curriculum (Luanrattana et al., 2012). The provision of mobile devices to adult learners by the institutions, however, will not necessarily increase the use of such devices by adult learners (Ellaway et al., 2014). In surgery education, augmented reality applications for smartphones and tablets have helped improve the authenticity in teaching and presenting research of surgical techniques (Atherton et al., 2013). Devices such as Personal Digital Assistants (PDAs) have facilitated workplace-based assessments by providing user-friendly platforms and a more structured framework compared to conventional paper-based modes (Coulby et al., 2011). The validity and reliability evidence of assessments using mobile devices are largely comparable to conventional workplace-based assessments. However, assessees may be anxious about potential technical issues when technology is used for assessment purposes (Deutsch et al., 2012). This has shown to be more among female assessees than male assessees and the anxiety related to potential technical lapses reduces substantially with the successful first launch.

Although this new technology offers the potential to enhance learning and patient care there are potential problems associated with its use. The informal and hidden curricula of mobile device use even in modern medical education is considerably negative (Ellaway, 2014). It is understandable as medicine and medical education are seriously lagging behind in adapting to major advancements in technology. According to Ellaway, the informal and hidden curricula are heavily influenced by perceptions of medical teachers and clinicians, perceptions of clinicians on their patients' perceptions, actual patient perceptions, and the perceptions of learners that is negative about using mobile devices. 'Not only are these various stakeholders unclear what is happening or what should happen, they are also second guessing each other's reactions thereby creating a tangled web of messages and influences that are clearly not contributing to a positive medical education environment' (Ellaway, 2014, p. 90), This may compromise the benefits of using mobile devices, particularly for point-of-care learning. The leadership in medical schools and healthcare organisations should set the agenda in this rapidly developing area to maximise the benefits of this powerful new technology while avoiding unintended consequences.

In Sri Lanka, although m-learning has been experimented with and used as a part of the formal curriculum, in other fields such as management for undergraduate education it is rare in medical education. However, as a very high percentage of adult learners have mobile devices with Internet connectivity, the potential of using m-learning for undergraduate medical education is vast. Mobile learning, however, is very common among postgraduate trainees. In postgraduate medical education, certain specialties offer online modules using LMSs. However, the scope is currently massively underutilised.

**Thinking point**: Perhaps as an adult educator you already use apps – how do you select and identify them? Have you and your adult learners identified other areas where apps would be useful? How might you take forward development and evaluation? (Ways identified include co-development with the adult learners, working with an IT faculty, and encouraging adult learners to share apps they have themselves found to be helpful.)

## Assessment

Assessment comes in three forms, and technology can enhance each. Diagnostic assessment can be used by you the adult educator or by the adult learners to assess how well an adult learner is doing at the start of a session. This can be done online, e.g. a quiz within the VLE, or at the start of a session via an audience response system such as *TurningPoint*™ or one using adult learners' own mobile devices such as *Poll Everywhere*™. Audience Response Technology (ART) in the context of healthcare education has been shown to enhance the classroom environment and motivation and promotion of adult learners for learning (Mostyn et al., 2012). Responses may be named or anonymous, and can also be used as a way of tracking adult learners' lecture attendance, e.g. by giving each new medical student their own *TurningPoint*™ handset which is not anonymised, allowing the school to track both attendance and performance on in-lecture testing.

Improving interactivity and providing feedback in large classes is a common challenge to all educators. Medical teachers have used technology to create games, enabling adult learners to self-assess their readiness for exams while interacting with their peers (Schlegel and Selfridge, 2014). Gaming elements can increase enjoyment of assessment, and reduce anxiety levels. Involving adult learners in preparing questions also deepens understanding of content.

Self-evaluation and formative learning can be enhanced by technology. In clinical skills, adult learners can be paired up, with one filming the other performing a clinical skill. Hawkins and colleagues (Hawkins et al., 2012) found that adult learners comparing their own performance with a 'gold standard' significantly improved their own self-evaluation skills. With the majority of adult learners now owning mobile devices with cameras, this is a cheap and effective learning opportunity. Adult learners can keep links to their videos in their portfolios to evidence development (links are encouraged rather than the video due to the size of videos). At postgraduate level, gamification (using the principles of game design to increase engagement) has attracted some interest, to harness medical trainees' competitiveness and motivate learning through quizzes delivered online. These are often completed outside work hours (Nevin et al., 2014).

Plagiarism detection software is increasingly used by institutions. This checks not only material available on the web but also it can check the institution's own assessment database. It can also be used formatively by adult learners to inform their understanding of academic integrity and writing.

Summative assessment increasingly relies on technology for its delivery, marking and storing results. Any assessment must be valid, reliable, acceptable, feasible and educationally effective (van der Vleuten and Schuwirth, 2005). With these in mind, the UK undergraduate courses have moved from the written open-question exam, long case and viva voce to MCQs (multiple choice questions), EMIs (extended matching items), OSCE (objective structured clinical examination), e-portfolio and simulation, and at trainee level, CbD (Case-based Discussion), mini-CEX (mini clinical evaluation exercise), DOPS (direct observation of procedural skills) and mini-PAT (mini-peer assessment tool) (Norcini and McKinley, 2007). MCQs and EMIs are delivered online in the UK, allowing efficient and quick marking and analysis of results. OSCEs are increasingly graded using hand-held devices, again allowing quick access to results and removing the risk of transfer/transcribing errors from when marks were hand-typed from examiners' hand-written sheets into the university assessment system.

Online portfolios are increasingly replacing paper-based ones, with their advantages of date-stamping, ease of accessibility and potential for including multi-media and hyperlinks. Feedback on trainee assessments allows easy access to previous feedback to the trainee and assessors, encouraging feed forward. In the UK the FY's progress is recorded in the FY's online portfolio, something they will maintain beyond the programme. In Japan, medical schools have become interested in introducing e-portfolios to their undergraduate medical education curriculum. Most advanced schools are using open-source platforms, such as MAHARA or SAKAI, and developing e-portfolio systems to support students' learning in their educational contexts. Developing e-portfolios for medical students is difficult, and many medical schools are struggling with it. The biggest challenge has been the need for staff who are both highly IT literate and can communicate with faculties in medical schools, most of whom are very busy with clinical work. After reforming its postgraduate training system, Japan introduced EPOC (which refers to the Evaluation system of postgraduate clinical training) (EPOC, 2015). Most of the teaching hospitals now use this tool and residents and supervisors there are asked to log in and fill in the evaluation form via a website.

Feedback can be written or audio, one to one or one to many. Hughes et al. (2008) describe the use of a webcam to enable staff to present feedback to a medical lecture without being in the lecture hall themselves. The Centre for Medical Education in Dundee uses an online reflective journal within the VLE for students to self-evaluate their assignments and enter into dialogue on the feedback. This has enhanced learning and reduced feelings of isolation among both adult learners and tutors on an online distance masters course (Ajjawi et al., 2013).

> **Thinking point**: How do you currently use technology to enhance your supervision, in particular creating a feedback dialogue with your adult learners? In what way do you explore possible changes / improvements to the process with your adult learners and colleagues?

## Conclusion

Technological advances are impacting both the working and educational practices in medical education. They bring challenges as well as benefits, e.g. professionalism lapses in the use of social networking against increased communication. Sharing resources and knowledge of processes within and across institutions is widespread, and in this chapter we have shared approaches from three quite different geographical settings within the same discipline area. Approaches to technology-enhanced learning may be different according to context, but what is universal is the ultimate aim of any medical training – to benefit the patient.

## Provocation

- In what ways do you currently use technology? Is it successful? From whose viewpoint?
- What new forms of technology could you now try?
- How might you evaluate the use of these technologies before, during and after implementing them to support adult learners?

## References

Ajjawi R., Schofield S., McAleer S. and Walker D. (2013). Assessment and feedback dialogue in online distance learning. *Medical Education*, 47(5), 527–528.

Alamro, A. S. and Schofield, S. (2012). Supporting traditional PBL with online discussion forums: A study from Qassim Medical School. *Medical Teacher*, 34(supl), S20–S24.

Alnabelsi, T., Al-Hussaini, A. and Owens, D. (2015). Synchronous e-Learning vs. face-to-face teaching using ENT emergencies as an educational intervention. *British Journal of Surgery*, 12, 206–206.

AMEE. (2014). Ming Jung Ho Symposium available at http://www.ameelive.org/2014/Ming_Jung_Ho_Symposium_7B_Day3_Video_Archive.php Accessed 16 May 2016/

The Asian Age (2012). Sri Lanka has more mobile phones per person, Retrieved Sept 9 2015 from http://www.lankanewspapers.com/news/2012/5/76256_space.html

Atherton, S., Javed, M., Webster, S. V. and Hemington-Gorse, S. (2013). Use of a mobile device app: A potential new tool for poster presentations and surgical education. *Journal of Visual Communication in Medicine*, 36(1-2), 6–10.

Australian Medical Council et al. (2010). Social media and the medical profession: A guide to online professionalism for medical practitioners and medical students, https://ama.com.au/sites/default/files/documents/Social_Media_and_the_Medical_Profession_FINAL_with_links_0.pdf Accessed 16 May 2016.

Baker, D. and Evans, W. (eds.), (2011). *Libraries and society: Role, responsibility and future in an age of change*. Philadelphia, US: Elsevier.

Bligh, J. (1995). Problem-based learning in medicine: An introduction. *Postgraduate Medical Journal*, 71(836), 323–326.

Bullock, A., Dimond, R., Webb, K., Lovatt, J., Hardyman, W. and Stacey, M. (2015). How a mobile app supports the learning and practice of newly qualified doctors in the UK: An intervention study. *BMC Medical Education*, 15(1, April), 71–77. DOI: 10.1186/s12909-015-0356-8

Cook, D. A., Brydges, R., Zendejas, B., Hamstra, S. J. and Hatala, R. (2013). Technology-enhanced simulation to assess health professionals: A systematic review of validity evidence, research methods, and reporting quality. *Academic Medicine*, 88(6), 872–883.

Cook, D. A., Hatala, R., Brydges, R., Zendejas, B., Szostek, J. H., Wang, A. T., ... and Hamstra, S. J. (2011). Technology-enhanced simulation for health professions education: A systematic review and meta-analysis. *Jama*, 306(9), 978–988.

Coulby C., Hennessey S., Davies N. and Fuller R. (2011). The use of mobile technology for work-based assessment: the student experience. *British Journal of Educational Technology*, 42(2), 251–265.

Daley, B. J. and Torre, D. M. (2010). Concept maps in medical education: An analytical literature review. *Medical Education*, 44(5), 440–448.

Davies, B. S., Rafique, J., Vincent, T. R., Fairclough, J., Packer, M. H., Vincent, R. and Haq, I. (2012). Mobile Medical Education (MoMEd) – how mobile information resources contribute to learning for undergraduate clinical students: a mixed methods study. *BMC Medical Education*, 12(1, January), 1. DOI: 10.1186/1472-6920-12-1.

DeCamp, M. (2013). Physicians, social media, and conflict of interest. *Journal of General Internal Medicine*, 28, 299–303.

Deutsch, T., Herrmann K., Frese T. and Sandholzer, H. (2012). Implementing computer-based assessment – A web-based mock examination changes attitudes. *Computers & Education*, 58, 1068–1075.

Ellaway, R. (2014). The informal and hidden curricula of mobile device use in medical education. *Medical Teacher,* 36(1), 89–91.

Ellaway, R. H., Fink, P., Graves, L. and Campbell, A. (2014). Left to their own devices: Medical learners' use of mobile technologies. *Medical Teacher*, 36(2), 130–138.

EPOC, (2015). EPOC (epoch) online postgraduate clinical training evaluation system. Retrieved 9 September 2015 from http://epoc.umin.ac.jp/

Ericsson, K. A. (2004). Deliberate practice and the acquisition and maintenance of expert performance in medicine and related domains. *Academic Medicine*, 79(10), S70–S81.

exMedio. (2015). exMedio. Retrieved 9 September 2015 from https://exmed.io/

Franko, O. I. and Tirrell, T. F. (2012). Smartphone app use among medical providers in ACGME training programs. *Journal of Medical Systems*, 36(5), 3135–3139.

General Medical Council. (2011). *Making and using visual and audio recordings of patients* GMC: London http://www.gmc-uk.org/Making_and_using_visual_and_audio_recordings_of_patients_2011.pdf_40338254.pdf

General Medical Council. (2013). *Confidentiality: Disclosing information for education and training purposes* GMC: London http://www.gmc-uk.org/Confidentiality_disclosingforeducation_Revised_2013.pdf_52091223.pdf

General Medical Council. (2015). *The foundation programme*. GMC: London http://www.foundationprogramme.nhs.uk/pages/home/training-and-assessment Accessed 16 May 2016.

Hawkins, S. C., Osborne, A., Schofield, S. J., Pournaras, D. J. and Chester, J. F. (2012). Improving the accuracy of self-assessment of practical clinical skills using video feedback – The importance of including benchmarks. *Medical Teacher*, 34(4), 279–284.

Holzinger, A., Nischelwitzer, A. and Meisenberger, M. (2005). Mobile phones as a challenge for m-Learning: Examples for Mobile Interactive Learning Objects (MILOs), *Proceedings of the 3rd International Conference on Pervasive Computing and Communications Workshops* (PerCom 2005 Workshops). pp. 307–311.

Hughes, C., Toohey, S. and Velan, G. (2008).eMed-Teamwork: A self-moderating system to gather peer feedback for developing and assessing teamwork skills. *Medical Teacher*, 30(1), 5–9.

Jaffar, A. A. (2012). YouTube: An emerging tool in anatomy education. *Anatomical Sciences Education*, 5(3), 158–164.

JISC (2013). Copyright Law for e-Learning authors. Retrieved 9 September 2015 from http://www.jisclegal.ac.uk/ManageContent/ViewDetail/ID/129/Copyright-Law-for-e-Learning-Authors-16-October-2013.aspx

JSIM (2015a). Meeting archives. Retrieved 9 September 2015 from http://www.naika.or.jp/meeting/nenji/nenji_archives/

JSIM (2015b). JSIM CPD tool. Retrieved 9 September 2015 from http://www.naika.or.jp/nintei/self/self_top/

Karnad, A. (2013). *Student use of recorded lectures: A report reviewing recent research into the use of lecture capture technology in higher education, and its impact on teaching methods and attendance.* Technical Report, London School of Economics and Political Science. Retrieved 9 September 2015 from http://eprints.lse.ac.uk/50929/

Kendall, M. and Enright, D. (2012). An agenda for UK clinical pharmacology: Provision of medicines information: The example of the British National Formulary. *British Journal of Clinical Pharmacology*, 73(6), 934–938.

Koehler, N., Vujovic, O. and McMenamin, C. (2013). Healthcare professionals' use of mobile phones and the Internet in clinical practice. *Journal of Mobile Technology in Medicine*, 2(1S), 3–13.

Kozu, T. (2006). Medical education in Japan. *Academic Medicine*, 81(12), 1069–1075.

Luanrattana, R., Win, K. T., Fulcher, J. and Iverson, D. (2012). Mobile technology use in medical education. *Journal of Medical Systems*, 36 (1, February), 113–122.

McCartney, M. (2012). How much of a social media profile can doctors have? *British Medical Journal*, 344: e440. DOI: http://dx.doi.org/10.1136/bmj.e440.

McGaghie, W. C., Issenberg, S. B., Cohen, M. E. R., Barsuk, J. H. and Wayne, D. B. (2011). Does simulation-based medical education with deliberate practice yield better results than traditional clinical education? A meta-analytic comparative review of the evidence. *Academic Medicine*, 86(6), 706.

McLaughlin, J. E., Roth, M.T., Glatt, D. M., Gharkholonarehe, N., Davidson, C. A., Griffin, L. M. and Mumper, R. J. (2014). The flipped classroom: A course redesign to foster learning and engagement in a health professions school. *Academic Medicine*, 89(2), 236–243.

Mostyn, A., Meade, O. and Lymn, J. S. (2012). Using audience response technology to provide formative feedback on pharmacology performance for non-medical prescribing students–a preliminary evaluation. *BMC Medical Education*, 12, 113. doi: 10.1186/1472-6920-12-113.

Nara, N., Beppu, M., Tohda, S. and Suzuki, T. (2009). The introduction and effectiveness of simulation-based learning in medical education. *Internal Medicine*, 48(17), 1515–1519.

Nevin, C. R., Westfall, A. O., Rodriguez, J. M., Dempsey, D. M., Cherrington, A., Roy, B., Patel, M. and Willig, J. H. (2014). Gamification as a tool for enhancing graduate medical education. *Postgraduate Medical Journal*, 90(1070), 685.

Norcini, J. J. and McKinley, D.W. (2007). Assessment methods in medical education. *Teaching and Teacher Education*, 23(3), 239–250.

Prober, C. G. and Khan, S. (2013). Medical education reimagined: A call to action. *Academic Medicine*, 88(10), 1407–1410.

Russomano, T., Cardoso, R. B., Fernandes, J., Cardoso, P. G., Alves, J. M., Pianta, C. D., Souza, H. P. and Lopes, M. H. I. (2009). Tele-surgery: A new virtual tool for medical education. *Studies in Health Technology Information*, 150, 866–870.

Schlegel, E. F. and Selfridge, N. J. (2014). Fun, collaboration and formative assessment: Skinquizition, a class wide gaming competition in a medical school with a large class. *Medical Teacher,* 36(5), 447–449.

Smith, R. (2012, December 6). The NHS will train fewer doctors to avoid future brain drain, report warns, *The Daily Telegraph.* Retrieved from http://www.telegraph.co.uk

Tam, C. W. M. and Eastwood, A. (2012). Available, intuitive and free! Building e-learning modules using web 2.0 services. *Medical Teacher*, 34(12), 1078–1080.

Tamblyn, R. M. (1980). Problem-based learning. An approach to medical education. In: H. Barrows and R. Tamblyn, (eds.), *Problem-based learning. An approach to medical education*. New York, USA: Springer.

Taradi, S. K., Taradi, M., Radić, K. and Pokrajac, N. (2005). Blending problem-based learning with Web technology positively impacts student learning outcomes in acid-base physiology. *Advances in Physiology Education*, 29(1), 35–39.

Traser, C. J., Hoffman, L. A., Seifert, M. F. and Wilson, A. B. (2015). Investigating the use of quick response codes in the gross anatomy laboratory. *Anatomical Sciences Education.* 8(5, September/October), 421–428.

van der Vleuten, C. P. and Schuwirth, L.W. (2005). Assessing professional competence: From methods to programmes. *Medical Education*, 39(3), 309–317.

Wallace, S., Clark, M. and White, J. ( 2012). 'It's on my iPhone': Attitudes to the use of mobile computing devices in medical education, a mixed-methods study. *BMJ* Open 22:e001099 DOI: 10.1136/bmjopen-2012-001099.

Chapter 8

# Shared objectives and communication

*Christine Redman and Deborah James*

## Introduction

This chapter explores research and practice in adult education through lenses of communication, behaviour, attitude and practice. It will consider ways to progress professional resilience and professional learning from the viewpoint of the adult educator. By describing some vignettes, the chapter considers how adult educators can achieve effective multi-agency work that builds an environment, language and ethos enabling adoption of the practices of others with wide ranging professional and community agendas.

This chapter first explains the background thinking that precedes the formation of a positive educative relationship with adults in different settings, through details of the theoretical background concepts that underpin the development and sustainment of effective learning relationships. Scenarios provided here have applicability to medical doctors, health professionals, teacher educators, and pre-service teachers, and are reported through an examination of a series of case studies.

Each group of participants will be explored through different types of interventions that were designed to explicitly progress the participants' knowledge and skill development. The theoretical framework references Positioning theory (Harré and van Langenhove, 1999) and Burkitt's (2002) modified version of Foucault's *Technologies of the self: Habitus and capacities*. The chapter references the contribution of words and actions that can help to create metaphors and support practical ways to empower reflective thinking.

Most professional learning approaches encompass ways to effectively enable the repositioning (Harré, 1991) and the empowering of individuals to more confidently enact themselves as both proactive and informed learners. Your adult learners in professional learning experiences should sense their increasing agency with any new specific targeted learning goals. Adult learners should come to understand how they are actively moving towards increasing their comprehension of the selected learning outcomes. These should be both useful and progressively move to more complex knowledge, understandings and skills. Adult learners, indeed all learners, require an offering of relevant, authentic and meaningful experiences. These may require extending from within a specific context, into alternative novel applied experiences. These moves can be supported by creativity and reflective experiences, like roleplay, journal writing or storytelling (see Chapter 3). However, implementation should have a resultant set of experiences that conclude with the adult learner being able to identify and explain how these new enhanced practices sustain her/his continued growth and effectiveness within a community of fellow adult learners.

The following examples provide vignettes from educational settings where the development of knowledge, skills and positive outcomes are important. The sites have similar goals at one level, but have different features that make them worthy of a closer examination. A common feature at each site was the need for members of the communities to work together. The desired goals of all required a strong sense of agreement and commitment to procure the outcomes. The basis of the impending change required that people came to hold similar institutional values and beliefs about the impending innovation. If similar values and beliefs had not been identified and established initially, then the targets for the projects would not have gained traction and be now flourishing. This is a challenge for projects of change, as they need to first establish shared understandings, language and agreements around key objectives.

What is often overlooked and can be under-valued is that when new projects or strategies are being introduced, time must be invested. This ensures everyone understands the goals, the reasons for the goals and the relationship of the goals to local needs. Time must be invested into unpacking and understanding the goals, so that people can relate to the goals. Adoption of the goals requires a commitment that cannot arise in a community if it is not accompanied by a shared understanding with the key stakeholders and those who will implement the changes.

This investment of time spent understanding the goals also serves to create a shared and common language in the community. It seems obvious and simplistic, yet time is a key factor. When people enter a learning space, where changes to practices are sought, participants require a clear understanding of the associated language and behaviours. Each adult programme described here commenced with time spent clarifying the goals. As project goals are developed and shared, prior assumptions and expectations arise. Assumptions and expectations warrant time for consideration and benefit from deliberation, as they underpin what people have already presupposed about the impending innovation or change. A false assumption can give birth to unexpected expectations and foil implementation processes.

## The notable role of assumptions and expectations that inform our everyday life

Assumptions arise from our everyday life. We make interpretations and form perceptions about our experiences. Assumptions inform many of our unreflected daily actions and form part of our everyday practices. We may be able to articulate our assumptions, but we are rarely required to do this unless our assumption fails to materialise in the way we had expected. Expectations arise from our assumptions and so assumptions create expectations.

When we enter a shop we assume there will be somebody there who will serve us. So when we enter a shop we are more likely to look around expectantly only when we are ready to be served, rather than when we first enter the shop.

Assumptions frequently exist tacitly, not stated or discussed they languish but actively inform our present and future behaviours. As adult educators our assumptions can influence what we 'do and say', and yet, we may remain unaware of their influence on our actions. Assumptions become very significant though, when institutional changes in practices are being sought. Assumptions influence what people expect. If people hold an assumption and it does not become realised as expected then disharmony and tension can occur. So, as the Chapter 6 in this book highlighted, as an adult educator it is worth investing time to establish which assumptions and expectations are influencing your adult learners' decisions and actions.

If you as an adult educator are unaware of your assumptions and how these are forming expectations, you may not know why you 'do what you do'. Likewise adult learners often need to be assisted to identify existing assumptions about their practices. Unpacking assumptions and expectations ensures that both the adult educator and the adult learner understand, examine, reflect on, and can modify tacit assumptions that can actively underpin unreflected habits.

## Introduction to an understanding of positions in a setting

The adult educators' and adult learners' position in a setting influences their capacity to be able to do and say certain things (Harré, 1991). Positioning theory makes clear how people may have adapted, adopted or challenged positions through their interpretation of their rights and duties.

An adult educator and the adult learner can assume, adopt or be allocated a position within a social grouping. The individual and other members of the community usually understand this position and its status. A position often aligns with an individual's role, but positions are distinctly different to the concept of 'role' (Harré, 1991). Role can be understood as stable and may be documented on paper. Positions vary and can do so moment by moment, and they may shift in response to people's perceptions of a conversation, and the accompanying do and say.

Adult educators and the adult learners may adopt and reject certain positions; however, what is significant here is that positions are dynamic and can shift and drift. Positions can be actively challenged and adult educators and the adult learners can actively attempt to re-position themselves or others. In the following examples the main aims were to support adults to consider specific modifications of their existing practices.

## Scenario 1: Positioning and re-positioning vignette

As an adult educator it is worth considering what you might have to do to establish participants in their current expertise, and ask yourself how will you use that foundation to set up a safe site for disruption as a mechanism for new learning?

The following historical vignette shows how re-positioning enabled and empowered a group to implement a change. In a school setting, teachers were considering investing a considerable amount of money into developing the computer infrastructure (Redman, 2008). The teachers argued instead for monies to be spent on music equipment, library books or play equipment. Rather than decree 'you will do this', the professional learning leader spent time supporting teachers to become familiar with the Department of Education's evidence of computers contributing to learning. Teachers were also supported to investigate other schools and to report back on any computer uses they valued. The teachers then acted as informed experts when making choices and sharing a more informed and inspired vision. They had acquired new, informed positions, and now had the language (the say), the experiences (the do), and had developed shared understandings (as a community of learners) to better inform their discussions, judgements and decision-making. Their previous assumptions and expectations of computers in schools had been changed. The school became a centre known for good practices, and catered for visitors from regional schools, who arrived to find a school where all teachers shared a commitment and language.

## Scenario 2: Examination of re-positioning in action in their social-cultural settings

This section focuses on three schools, all primary or elementary schools desiring change in practices. First, Silver Lake primary school sought to redevelop their whole-school science curriculum.

Second, Cooper Lane primary school requested that their teaching staff use personalised learning in their classroom teaching approaches. This was introduced to teachers experientially, through the development of their own personalised collegiately negotiated learning goals.

Third, Bronze Beach primary school wanted to implement a whole-school teaching approach. These teachers were to become successful at enacting supportive strategies. The implementation was to be led by a special team.

Introducing a change into an adult group of professionals who are already proficient and deem themselves to be operating well will always require care, respect and thorough planning.

## Background principles to the introduction of a change

You as an adult educator implementing change first need to understand the underlying informing principles and import of the innovation. You will need to experience it, trial it, discuss and explore it with peers. It will be calibrated against existing assumptions and expectations and determined as fit, or not, for purpose.

People can be supported to be exploratory, curious and questioning, and actively positioned to be wondering and pondering, 'what happens if and when?' It can be supportive for adults to be titled as learners. This acts as re-positioning and can assist the taking up of new positions. The title change to 'learners' provides opportunities for them to change what they do and say. The attributes of learners include asking questions. Questions support the development of shared language, and help to provide clarity about what will be different and what will be expected of them in practice. In this process, people come to align their existing assumptions, expectations, values, and beliefs, connecting these to the refined expectations and practices.

Identifying and helping people to establish their existing assumptions is critical in a change process. Your assumptions and your adult learners' assumptions and expectations align with personal and professional beliefs and values. So communities too need to understand their pervasive existing assumptions and expectations, and how these align with their institutional beliefs and values and the newer expectations.

At any site, over time, practices develop, refine, are adapted, replicated, and passed on. In time, these practices are no longer discussed, now tacit and perhaps reified, and eventually they become difficult to examine or contest. Practices become part of the habitus forming the local umwelt.

Institutional sites are socio-cultural psychological spaces where you as an adult educator and your adult learners make choices and have the capacity to implement change or derail it. Positioning theory recognises the rights and duties of individuals and acknowledges the implications of the local order on people's agential behaviours (Harré and van Langenhove, 1999).

Adult educator's rights and duties in a workplace are often well known to the individual as they are formally documented and written into policy level artifacts. These could include a duty to work an eight-hour day and the right to have a morning tea and lunch break. However, you as an adult educator will also need to be aware of rights and duties that are not made explicit, but are implicit and well known and enacted minute by minute. These rights and duties could be understood by thinking about a person entering a staff room. They might assume there will be teacups and drinking glasses, chairs and possibly tables, access to hot water, a refrigerator, sandwich toaster and microwave oven. These objects are symbols of their rights and these rights come with duties. Duties could include shutting the refrigerator door, returning cups to the sink, or removing dirty lunch plates from the tearoom on completion of their meal. These examples indicate how assumptions easily become everyday expectations.

However, there is another layer of rights and duties, a deeper layer, much less visible in the environment than a cup and chair. These rights and duties are aligned with the moral and ethical rights members of an adult education community can reasonably expect. Rights and duties could include assuming you have a 'voice', an expectation of being heard, and knowing your ideas have been heard. Adult learners in learning scenarios require opportunities for voice, and signs that they have been heard and their ideas considered.

An adult learner needs to hear his or her own voice. As one's own voice, one's words are representative of one's thinking, understandings and values. The latent assumptions and expectations need airing. Meanings are constructed in the dialectic, in the conversational interactions with others; this is how meaning is made, and shared understandings are developed (Redman, 2008; Redman and Fawns, 2010).

Adult learning communities seeking shared understandings and practices need to note the significance of the voice and utilise strategies that create opportunities for voices to be heard. Hearing one's voice involves reflecting on one's thinking (see Chapter 3). When implementing learning experiences and opportunities for change in practices, it is essential to use the language related to the innovation. Conversations support the identification of existing ideas, connect related ideas, and highlight what has not been considered, believed and/or valued. The following strategies support individuals by providing time for them to reflect on their thinking and identify useful language, and perhaps signal existing assumptions and expectations.

## Personal meaning-making maps (PMM maps)

As an adult educator it is worth considering how you will ensure that your adult learning activity is designed to enable participants to stop and think. It is worth thinking about what methods you could reliably use to develop participants' curiosity in their current work practices and context.

One strategy you could use is personal meaning-making maps (PMM maps) (Falk and Needham, 2013; Giardiello et al., 2013). The title flags that this is personal and can be private. However, they can also be shared, and can become a community sense-making exercise. When introducing a change of practices or a new innovation, the adult educator and the adult learner require time. This time is needed to ponder the known and the usefulness of existing understandings to the newer and less familiar world. Strategies like PMM maps help to make explicit the known so that as adult learners they can more intentionally target the less known.

A PMM map increases awareness of what one knows and what one does not know or understand. This can support curiosity and elicit questions. It becomes indicative of an adult learner's current breadth of knowledge, depth of understanding, and related ideas and experiences. A PMM map signals the degree of commitment to an idea and how well an idea aligns with someone's values.

The PMM maps can remain private and personal, but they can also be shared, and made public and social.

A PMM map makes clear to adult learners and educators what they know and understand, and identify the existing links and connections to related topics or foci. The unknown and less familiar are made more readily identifiable. PMM maps alert the map-maker to what might be novel elements creating clarity about known and unknown ideas. This also helps to position people as learners.

PMM maps are more often experienced as an individual activity. They have the potential to be shared and discussed with a group. In the action of sharing one's thinking, in words, with another, a conversation arises and meanings and interpretations are exchanged. They suit times when pairs are working together to probe their understandings as they help to develop shared language and ideas.

Sharing with one other person, after identifying one's current knowledge and ideas, is a less risky activity than stating one's ideas to a group. Every adult learner needs time to think, reflect on, and locate the appropriate associated words and a PMM map can aid this process. When adult learner pairs share their PMM map, much affirmation occurs in the first few minutes of sharing, before they venture into the high-risk areas comprised of less familiar areas. Then the pairs will ask questions of each other and ideas move from the private space to the social and public space.

If a change – an innovation – is to be undertaken and implemented, it will require establishing shared visions and understandings, and most significantly, a shared language.

A shared language is vital as it is in the language, in the words that associated meanings are created and ideas and values can be shared. Words communicate ideas, and can pre-empt and avoid miscommunication and inaccurate assumptions. It helps to form common aims that subsequently provide participants with confidence. It shares power and ensures adult educators and adult learners more willingly contribute. It develops trust and enables all to feel like informed members of a community.

## Collaborative Interactive Discussions (CID)

It is worth reflecting on and developing strategies to help you as an adult educator activate increased awareness of assumptions that underpin participant practice. For when a new theoretical idea or practice is being introduced, adult educators and adult learners need to engage with and understand the informing principles. A person's professional learning can be better supported when s/he understands the underpinning theory (see Chapter 4). Once the broader overarching principles are understood, adult learners often adapt the principles to their more local site's needs.

Individuals and dyads benefit from their local community conversations. Once an individual's thinking has been documented, reflected on and shared, these ideas can be shared within the immediate collective. The enabling tool recommended here is a Collaborative Interactive Discussion known as a CID (Giardiello et al., 2014).

The CID acts as a mechanism to shift assumptions and expectations within a collective using dialogue. It is imperative that adult learners within a collective are able to successful identify and negotiate contradictions and any conflicts that might exist. As an adult educator you need to consider how you could make the interactional and emotional labour entailed in dealing well with conflict an attractive focus for participants. A CID is a tool that provides community members with information and opportunities to converse with others. A key strength of the CID is that it ensures everyone has a voice. Every person has time and an opportunity to express ideas and to hear others' ideas.

In terms of the strategy, the CID provides adult learners and adult educators with background information, usually a few short sentences about the topic. This information comes from a key authority. Then a question related to this information is asked, 'What might some of the implications for our community be if this was implemented?' People respond in writing limited to a sentence or two. They pass this sheet of paper to the person on their right, and simultaneously receive a sheet of paper from the person on their left. It may have a different statement and question. They read the responses and write a response to the person's statements. In groups of four to six people, this process continues until the sheet returns to the original person. Then time is given to read and discuss the insights as shared before them.

After time has been given to write, read, respond, and read and write, adult learners and adult educators have the opportunity to be heard and to understand the thinking of others. It is not uncommon for people to state that this is the first time they have heard the thinking of so many of their peers.

A CID can take many forms, and can serve many purposes. It will contribute to the creation of a shared language, to an understanding of the thinking of others, and to the development of visions. It helps to create a community of adult learners and educators who understand the goals and visions of others so they can learn *with* each other, *from* each other and *for* each other.

## PMM maps and CIDs and communities of learners in action

Back to our earlier scenario: Silver Lake, Cooper Lane and Bronze Beach primary schools each sought to implement an initiative that required the commitment of all participants. It was essential everyone had the time to fully investigate the change, and consider the ramifications for themselves and for the areas for which they were responsible.

The programmes were implemented over a year. Drawing on the experiences of the three schools we suggest that adult educators intending to adopt a similar approach ensure that time is given to meet regularly throughout the year. Ensure a leadership team is available to support the daily demands of the implementation.

Begin with a clarification about the initiative. Then, provide think time for adult learners to complete a personal PMM map. Ensure there is time to share this with another adult learner, and then share as a dyad their thinking with another dyad. Each group of four can then report on the significant elements of its discussion. In particular, each group could be asked the question, 'What was interesting and or surprising to you about your conversations?' This focus on 'interesting or surprising' asks adult learners to reflect on what was new or novel to them in their discussions. It does not encourage a 'down pat' answer; rather, it encourages sharing of the unfamiliar and often what has been learned. It provides for the development of a supportive community of adult learners. This works to actively re-position adult community members as adult learners. These adult learners are sharing novel information. They are aware of their self and their known world, and can act to progress themselves as a work in progress (Burkitt, 2002) as the learning required becomes visible to them.

## Scenario 3: In-patient case study vignette

In this example, training was designed for staff working in an in-patient hospital setting for people with a learning disability who also had challenging behaviours. The intervention was adapted from a United Kingdom, National Institute of Clinical Excellence recommended intervention (National Institute for Health and Clinical Excellence, 2013) that uses video feedback with individuals: Video Interaction Guidance (VIG; see Kennedy et al., 2011). The new training was delivered to teams of mental health nurses and nursing assistants. All members of the team worked with the same patient.

The concept of the parallel process was the major underpinning premise of the training. Therefore design principles included:

- organising training around each participant's hopes and desires for change to enable them to appreciate the specific personal needs, hopes and desires of patients, with potential for their own work to be organised more centrally around the patient;
- exposing the participants' expertise, showing the value of their lived experience and how the knowledge of their lived experience contributes to a collective meaning construction which would enable staff to appreciate the perspective of others in the development of knowledge.

These design principles were embedded in interaction. Interaction between the trainer and the participants was modelled, and interaction was also made the explicit focus of the training through the act of video recording in-situ practice, editing and analysing interactional turns between participants and between the participants and the patient. Using video playback enables a micro-analysis of interpersonal behaviour. This means that the expression of emotion and thought, which is complex, simultaneous and fast in real time, can be systematically analysed. A micro-analysis of video footage, when viewed through an appreciative lens, can provide a constructive space to:

- test pre-existing judgements about interpersonal capacity, capability and patterns of success for a patient;
- construct more in-depth understanding of the impact of behaviour on patient, staff and family relationships;
- challenge pre-existing beliefs and attributions that may become normalised around a patient by a staff team.

Drawing on the experience from this example, we suggest that staff attend two half-day workshops delivered within one week. They take video recordings of themselves in interaction with the patient during the days between the workshops. Staff members can then be interviewed as part of an evaluation of the new workshop by an independent researcher.

In our example in the interviews before the workshop the participants were patient-focused. They expressed a desire to understand the inner workings of the patient and linked that to their ability to diffuse challenging behaviour and recognised that this would be beneficial to the patient. In the interviews that followed the workshops there was a shift of perspective. They were now talking about themselves and their colleagues and the inner workings of themselves had become a legitimate and celebrated focus of attention.

## Summary

Institutions are complex places. They have reified practices developed over time, and daily reproduce these known practices. Changing clinicians or teachers' well-established practices can be problematic. Clinicians and teachers are hesitant to replace well-known and productive practices with untried practices that need time to refine and then use effectively. Time spent understanding approaches helps to make clear key underlying principles that drive the change. This ensures that adults as learners understand the importance of changes, and can develop both a personal and a collegiate impetus.

## Provocation

As an adult educator:

- How will you ensure that participants have the space to hear their own voice as they are guided to take a step back?
- How will you ensure that those assumptions are disrupted in a way that gives rise to generative outcomes?
- How will you enable participants to see how position, not role, may determine the potential for expanded practice?
- How will you model the use of conflict in the learning context to increase appreciation in the participants of others' perspectives?
- How will you monitor the establishment of continuity in participants' past representations of knowledge and their new formulations of knowledge?

## References

Burkitt, I. (2002). Technologies of the self: Habitus and capacities. *Journal for the Theory of Social Behaviour*, 32(2), 219–237.

Falk, J. H. and Needham, M. D. (2013). Factors contributing to adult knowledge of science and technology, *Journal of Research in Science Teaching*, 50(4), 431–452.

Giardiello, P., Parr, N. McLeod, R. and Redman, C. (2014). Understanding pedagogy. In S. Rodrigues (ed.), *Handbook for teacher educators: Transfer, translate or transform* (pp. 15–33). Rotterdam, The Netherlands: Sense Publishers.

Harré, R. (1991). The discursive production of selves. *Theory and Psychology*, 1(1), 51–63.

Harré, R. and van Langenhove, L. (1999). *Positioning theory: Moral contexts of intentional action.* Oxford, England: Blackwell.

Kennedy, H., Landor, M. and Todd, L. (eds.), (2011). *Video interaction guidance: A relationship-based intervention to promote attunement, empathy and wellbeing.* London: Jessica Kingsley.

National Institute for Health and Clinical Excellence. (2013). *Autism: the management and support of children and young people on the autistic spectrum.* NICE clinical guidance 170. Retrieved from www.nice.org.uk/cg170

Redman, C. (2008). *The research planning meeting.* In R. Harré, F. Moghaddam and N. Lee (eds.), *Global conflict resolution through positioning analysis* (pp. 95–112). New York, NY: Springer.

Redman, C. and Fawns, R. (2010). How to use pronoun grammar analysis as a methodological tool for understanding the dynamic lived space of people. In S. Rodrigues (ed.), *Using analytical frameworks for classroom research* (pp. 163–182). New York, NY: Routledge.

Chapter 9

# Developing teams

## Boring title, interesting case studies, great outcomes!

*Paul Edwards, Brian Rock and Elizabeth Gibson*

### A note on terminology

The term 'manager' is used in this chapter to represent anyone who has the responsibility of leading and/or developing people under them, regardless of the size of their team or their organisational role.

### Introduction

Developing and leading teams provides myriad challenges for an individual, whether they are a first-time team leader or an experienced executive. Many factors come into play – unique to each situation – that preclude a single formula for successfully developing teams. Some of these factors are (and include the manager):

- The personalities of each individual in the team. Recognising that all people are individuals, and differences between individuals exist.
- Positive and negative experiences that are carried by all individuals as 'baggage' and predicate how they will react to similar situations in future.
- Communication capabilities between team members. A more nuanced approach than 'one-size-fits-all' to team communications is better.
- The motives of team members. A challenge for the manager is to understand and articulate outcomes the team has to achieve and make sure these outcomes are aligned with individual outcomes being sought by team members.
- The manager's ability to take on board feedback and ensure that the feedback is considered, and seen to be considered. This does not mean that the feedback need be applied, merely that the team sees that an authentic effort has been given to consider the feedback.
- The context in which the team operates. This context may be one or more of the organisational hierarchy context, organisational culture, the situational context, legislative or regulatory constraints, and the team's (or organisation's) financial context (including shareholder considerations and stock market conditions, if applicable), as well as other contexts.

This chapter presents three mini case studies, which explore the above themes. The mini case studies all provide a problem statement to set the scene and context. The first two mini case studies (Paul Edwards, Elizabeth Gibson) provide a description of the approach taken to solve issues encountered, and the outcomes achieved. The third mini case study (Paul Edwards, Brian Rock and Elizabeth Gibson) describes a situation where the team's manager is unable or unwilling to provide clear, firm, and decisive leadership.

It is our intent and hope that these mini case studies provide you, as an adult educator, with clear and illustrative examples of techniques for you to adapt and adopt for challenges you may face in developing and leading teams.

## Case study 1: Time

### *Problem statement*

The global organisation in question was reaching the end of an onerous three-year contract. The IT services provided under the contract could only be changed with the involvement of lawyers. The services provided were in a dynamic and rapidly shifting context. Additionally, it was believed within the organisation that the services being provided could be provided internally at less cost, providing the services were delivered offshore.

Paul was provided with the following brief: set up a facility offshore providing the same or better level of service, within six months (the contract expiry date).

Paul assembled a team of seven subject matter specialists (who would be working on this in addition to their day jobs) and outlined the requirement. The response from the room was unanimous: six months was not long enough. Several people in the room commented that previous experience of setting up a similar facility required at least 12 months with people working full time on it.

How could the uniform negativity in the room be turned around? Could the requirement be achieved in six months?

### *Approach*

Each person in the room was asked to precisely articulate their concerns – what were the specific barriers these experts saw in achieving the objective in six months? The focus of the discussion was around time rather than any other dimension: no one in the room doubted their ability to deliver without the time constraint. These were captured on writeable walls until all objections to the timings had been documented.

Paul then acknowledged the objections, and thanked everyone for providing them.

'But – just imagine if we did do it! How cool would that be?'

There was a murmur of agreement within the room, before someone raised a time-based objection. Paul responded by asking that staff member how they would feel if they managed to achieve it.

The discussion continued until one of the staff members said, 'You know, perhaps we could fully document the processes if we had a good template. Does anyone have one?'

Paul had one, and supplied it. Paul then asked if there was anything else he could provide to assist in reducing or eliminating the documented objections. In the end, the only time-based objections left were to do with the physical build of the facility (due to the nature of the function being provided, there were some special physical requirements), and obtaining regulatory approvals. Paul asked if there was a minimum build that would be acceptable and achievable within six months, and two of the subject matter experts agreed to define what these requirements would look like.

Paul concluded the session by thanking the participants for their contribution and enthusiasm, finishing with 'Just imagine being part of delivering this!'

A schedule was developed and shared for comment among the team. It was tight: in six months there was just six days of slack (and that was based around some heroic assumptions). Paul made it clear that if the team members needed anything, he was available to assist: helping with the work (where technically possible), doing menial tasks to support the experts, working around roadblocks within the organisation.

Paul approached a regulatory compliance group and outlined the situation. A plan was developed to obtain as many approvals as possible in the six-month period.

## *Outcome*

The function was operational and running two weeks early! The team worked above and beyond what Paul expected. When a debriefing session was conducted after the new function had gone live, several team members commented that the project was fun, challenging, and rewarding. When asked why they had contributed so much energy over a 22-week period to the project, several themes stood out. The team:

- believed in the purpose of the project;
- felt Paul never demanded of them, but asked;
- frequently took Paul up on his offer of help, and it was always applied. One team member noted that he lifted his quality standards once Paul had provided some assistance, and the team member saw the improvement in his output.

None of the team had technical writing backgrounds. One team member of a non-English speaking background was asked to document the process. He accepted, provided he could withdraw if he felt he was not doing a good job. He has subsequently enrolled in further education around technical writing as he enjoyed it so much.

## *Positives*

The following points have come from feedback solicited from team members:

- **Letting people vent and the power of imagination**
The team was allowed to fully express their concerns about the project. This removed the negativity from people, and allowed individuals to articulate in detail the nature of their concerns, and then work creatively to reduce or eliminate them. However, the key lesson is that imagination got them over the line at the start! Letting the team imagine what it would *feel* like to achieve the outcome changed their mindsets about what was possible.
- **Pacesetting by the leader**
The team took up Paul's offer to assist in working toward the outcome. This provided three outcomes in terms of motivating the team: quality, commitment, and reduction of the power gradient in the team. Paul produced work that showed the level of quality he expected from the team; the team members adjusted their output accordingly. The team members felt as though the author was committed to achieving the outcome, through a willingness to 'roll up [his] sleeves'. Finally, Paul providing work and soliciting feedback on the content and quality reduced the power gradient in the team. The team members felt that Paul was 'one of [them]' through this action.
- **Asking politely is better than demanding**
Both the team members and the regulatory compliance group provided feedback that asking rather than demanding created an inclusive environment that motivated better work. The project required regulatory approvals from 32 jurisdictions globally, with some requiring nine months to grant approvals! The regulatory compliance group member who joined the team spent considerable professional capital in pushing approval through faster than normal. Paul asked this person why he had acted in this way, given that they had never met before. The reply was: 'It's simple. You asked, politely, rather than demanded. I wanted to help you'.

## *Pitfalls to avoid*

The following points have come from feedback solicited from team members:

- **Some people are uncomfortable with autonomy**
Due to the nature and context of the project, Paul gave broad direction, and left it to individual team members to determine the best way to achieve their specific outcomes. Within the first week, two of the seven team members separately and repeatedly approached the author for assistance. Paul was mystified with the seemingly trivial nature of what was being asked. After discussion, it was determined that these were the two least experienced members of the team, and were unused to being given so much autonomy.

A change in approach with these two members to provide more explicit direction moved these two team members back into their comfort zones. Earlier recognition and change of approach would have made the first fortnight of the project more comfortable for these two team members.

- **There is always time for analysis**
  An analysis of the team's approach, including scheduling and task definition, was performed as part of the debriefing session. Three of the tasks were found to have been incorrectly defined, adding several days' effort to the project. All of the tasks were the accountability of one of the two junior staff members. A priori analysis to avoid this extra work would have taken two hours, but did not occur due to the time pressure felt by the team at the start of the project.

## Case study 2: A government laboratory

### *Problem statement*

Elizabeth's mini case study has an all too familiar context: a newly elected government was intent on downsizing and outsourcing non-core functions. A government department contained a laboratory. The CEO of the department saw the laboratory as a key function to the organisation that undertook prosecutions for enforcement purposes and was adamant that it should be kept. The CEO, having previously managed the laboratory many years before, appeared to hold a somewhat rose-tinted view of its past performance. The laboratory was suffering from poor morale after an aggressive internal audit had focused on commercial laboratory performance indicators as a benchmark. Understanding the difference in work between commercial and government laboratories is required in order to appreciate the effect this audit finding would have on staff morale.

Routine work was outsourced to commercial laboratories. The key difference between the commercial and government laboratories is that commercial laboratories are driven by profit (through low-margin high-throughput routine work). Most of this work would be automated or undertaken by technicians (non-graduates). The government laboratory focused on analysis of complex mixtures of unidentified chemicals in different matrixes with the results used for prosecutions, hence, analysis needed to be undertaken by suitably qualified personnel, such as those with graduate degrees in chemistry. In consultation with commercial laboratories it became apparent they viewed the samples received by the government laboratory as non-routine and would be unable to complete the analysis in the same time as routine samples.

Additionally, the government laboratory had recently appointed a young female laboratory manager, having successfully obtained the role ahead of two of the three senior male staff. In an atmosphere of fear over retrenchments the laboratory had become the butt of jokes in the department.

Finally, the laboratory had a dysfunctional structure and a serious lack of direction. The direction of the laboratory was set by the department's executive including the CEO who was influenced by negative news headlines that changed almost daily and had led to numerous unfinished projects in the laboratory.

Where to from here?

## Approach

The new laboratory manager had a background in industry rather than government, where the drivers were much more financially focused: perform or the company would go belly up. In government, the drivers are somewhat different: less focus on financial performance and more driven by a Minister keeping pace with the news and wanting immediate action, especially if there was likely to be a negative impact on the opinion polls. The reputation of the department and, hence, budget allocation would depend on the satisfaction or dissatisfaction of the Minister. Satisfaction did not necessarily mean an increased budget though the CEO generally gets to keep her/his job!

The new manager of the laboratory undertook a five-step approach to fixing the issues. The first step undertaken by the new manager was to meet with the senior laboratory staff individually and allow them to vent – which they did vehemently!

Second, she met with all staff to dispel the fear of retrenchment (admittedly some staff may have been looking forward to being retrenched!) and setting an agreed-to objective: that they were going to aim to be the best performing government laboratory in the country, which appeared to hit the right note (albeit with some degree of skepticism).

Third, the current structure of the laboratory (comprising 15 staff) was dysfunctional with various classic examples of poor organisational behaviour:

- one section distanced themselves from the rest of the laboratory;
- two of the senior staff were not communicating well with each other; and
- the hierarchical structure meant there was little respect for experienced technical staff.

The laboratory manager sought and received approval from the Executive and CEO for two key actions: rearranging the organisational structure; and re-arranging the physical structure of the laboratory. Both of these actions, especially the first one, had to be executed in the context of a highly-unionised workforce.

What followed was a rearranged structure that was team-based and combined and co-located those sections that were conducting similar functions. With respect to the co-location a budget and broad parameters were given to work to by the laboratory manager with the staff deciding on how the implementation would actually take place. The co-location was undertaken with the aim of improving productivity through improved staff communication (e.g. problem solving). An added bonus of this change in physical space would be for staff morale to improve, but it was felt that the improved communication would be benefit enough from the relocation programme.

Fourth, in order to foster the right ethos among team members, some team building took place outside of the laboratory. The team building constituted command tasks with cognitive and physical problems where there were a multitude of solutions, and introducing principles of high reliability such as 'sensitivity to operations' and 'deference to expertise'.

Finally, the myriad of projects that were playing havoc with productivity were reviewed. They were seen as 'more fun and having higher kudos' than other laboratory work by staff, but nonetheless were culled, in consultation with staff and customers, in favour of a smaller number of higher value projects. Additionally, a simplified project management template was introduced. Project progress was reported on a weekly basis with parameters of targets achieved and budget expended being recorded.

## Outcome

The turnaround in the performance of the laboratory was remarkable. Within a matter of months, the laboratory was demonstrating increased productivity; a greatly improved completion rate of projects; an improved success ratio in terms of grant funding for projects; and improved credibility within the department and the media.

These achievements were only made possible through the active engagement of staff in a team-focused process. Several aspects of the manager's approach stand out in terms of leading to this success. These may be of interest to other adult educators:

- Co-location drives better communication – Ensuring that the physical structure of the team better represented how the various sub-groups within the team behaved and interacted removed impediments to clear communication and collaborative problem solving.
- Clear objectives were set by the staff, not just the manager – The objective that was set came about as a result of team discussion. In addition, the objective was simple, making it easy for new staff who were not present at the objective-setting session to understand and embrace how the laboratory understood itself and what it (and its staff) believed was possible.
- Clear communication with staff – Weekly meetings were held with staff at the beginning of the week where performance was reported and discussed in addition to safety being put on the agenda. These meetings ensured that all issues could be aired, and contributed to the improvement in staff morale.
- Letting staff know how they were performing as a team provides opportunities for motivation – The laboratory manager set up a committee consisting of similar government laboratory managers drawn countrywide in order to undertake a benchmarking exercise. Performance objectives were identified

that were realistic and communicated to the CEO and Executive team as well as to the laboratory staff. Benchmarking was also carried out against commercial laboratories, however, the original performance objectives that had been identified in the audit were for routine analysis only and, as these were already outsourced, were irrelevant to the government laboratory.

- Understanding what is important to staff helps with morale and retention – The salary paid to public servants is generally lower than in industry with not much room for pay increases. However, there was the option of undertaking further study, which was actively encouraged by the manager.
- Performance objectives must be aligned with operational objectives and be relevant to the context – The laboratory manager participated in developing a performance assessment process for the government department that was subsequently implemented The laboratory staff focused on team objectives, performance outcomes and customer service.

## Case study 3: Corporate sociopath

In this mini case study Brian provides an example that highlights what does not work – for knowing what does not work is as important as knowing what works. This case study contains details of an approach that adult educators are advised not to adopt!

### *Problem statement*

Failure can be instructive.

A newly-appointed research director had worked for outstanding managers, and poor ones, with few in the middle. His latest manager, unfortunately, belonged to the second set. The company was successful on many business metrics: large, profitable and high profile. However, it struggled to retain staff, or grow the business, and was widely regarded as a poor place to work.

The research director reported to the managing director, who was excellent at skills required lower down in the organisation: an outstanding business writer, a solid financial manager, with a good sense of process. When it came to developing high-performance teams, he was a spectacular failure.

The research director's principles for leading teams were simple: establish and communicate clear objectives, and provide as much direction as needed (and no more) to enable team members to deliver on these, and reinforce positives.

The principles used by this manager were the antithesis of providing unclear and inconsistent direction, micromanaging the work, and being unremittingly negative about the results. Expanding on this in more detail there are a number of *anti-lessons* one can observe. For knowing what not to do is as important as knowing what to do.

What follows below are examples of what not to do:

*1. Never provide a coherent brief.*

The research director was often called in to the manager and given a verbal brief. Follow up emails to clarify went unanswered. The research director believed he understood the requirements, only to submit work and be told it was completely wrong due to additional criteria that were not previously discussed.

Inevitably it took two or three attempts to finally produce work that was considered acceptable. It was common for the objectives and scope to completely change from the time work began until it was delivered. It's one thing to move the goal posts. It's another to keep them in constant motion.

*2. Micromanage as negatively as possible.*

Providing detailed oversight is not always a bad thing, especially for people new to an organisation, or in a new role, who may require a high degree of direction. It is less useful for routine tasks that simply do not require high levels of supervision, and counterproductive when the staff member has a higher level of expertise than the micromanager.

Consider the example of a weekly two-page report. It took two or three months to sort out the content, format and style, for what was fundamentally a very simple, straightforward task. Each week's initial drafts invariably provoked waves of criticism. After a few months of this the self-doubt created serious productivity problems. It led to constant second-guessing, which led to longer turnaround times in selecting material and writing it up. The eventual work-around solution was to submit work as late as possible. This would prompt criticism for leaving work to the last minute.

*3. Ask for honest opinions and then punish staff for providing such information.*

As noted earlier the company had a serious staff retention problem. Turnover was much higher than normal for the industry, especially for junior staff. The research director had spoken at length with a number of the junior colleagues. Their experiences were consistent: long hours, massive workloads, severe deadline pressure and no strong sense of the company being interested in their well-being or future career development. Unfortunately the research director received a dressing down after he was asked for and fed back the junior colleagues' views.

*4. Don't train your staff. That's their responsibility.*

At one point the research director proposed conducting a series of training sessions to teach the younger staff core skills useful in their current jobs, and providing them with the level of analytical skills they would need at higher levels. Authorisation was given, on the proviso the sessions were run out of working hours. The manager stated that career development was in the employee's interest, and therefore the employee's responsibility. Providing a venue for instruction in the workplace was sufficient investment on the company's part, and considered more than was warranted given most of the staff would be gone within two years. The sessions were organised before work and during lunchtimes. Enthusiasm was poor: there was a weak turn-out for the first two or three sessions, which soon dribbled away to nothing.

The research director later discussed this with a manger in another organisation which had a strong staff-development programme. Their perspective was 'some companies worry about investing in staff training, saying, "what if we train them and they leave?" Our attitude is, "what if we don't train them and they stay, what are the consequences?"'

Of course training is only one factor that retains staff. Recognition for contributions is another, providing a segue to anti-lesson five.

*5. Steal ideas.*

A big de-motivator is having work appropriated by a superior. For example, two weeks after an idea was pitched to a reluctant managing director, the managing director re-pitched the research director's own idea back at him. It is possible the manager did not actually mean to steal the idea: he may have forgotten the original discussion, absorbed the idea, and genuinely thought that it was his own.

*6. Disempower your people.*

All the decisions made by the research director, no matter how small, had to be approved by the managing director, and were usually amended on principle.

Disempowering people can take place when discussions are started negatively. For example a managing director who begins a discussion about a project due that afternoon with the words 'as usual I expect you've done nothing about it' is unlikely to empower people, especially if the project is completed and on the manager's desk.

Strong leadership is important, but some managers confuse strong leadership with obsessive control. After changing his job the research director took on a similar role, but for a manager who created a positive environment that motivated staff, provided clear objectives, and focused on deliverables instead of process. That led to a long, productive, and satisfying period of employment.

## Overview

The mini cases provide a stark and instructive contrast, which highlight the importance of the key factors that lead to motivated teams that produce high-quality work. These factors include:

- providing clear briefs;
- giving staff confidence and opportunity to focus on producing useful work;
- encouraging open and honest communications;
- providing training and development;
- giving credit, and generally empowering staff to be actively engaged in making decisions that work in the organisation's interests.

## Conclusion

Despite the different contexts and imperatives in the three mini case studies, some themes stand out. Describing these is relatively simple, understanding how you would apply them to a specific context is the challenging part.

Consider the first theme in this conclusion: allowing adult learners/staff to 'vent' and get issues off their chests. In the first two case studies this worked, but it is a fine balance. Vent for too long and a sense of negativity pervades the team, as people start to believe the negativity. Conversely, cutting the discussion too soon may mean team members feel that they are not being given a fair say, or the effort to understand the issues is not authentic.

### *Allow adult learners/staff to express their feelings honestly and safely*

Ensuring that adult learners/staff can express how they feel is as important, if not more so than ensuring adult learners/staff express what they are thinking. A safe environment for this is vital. Getting the balance right here is hard: too much negativity can pervade the team, but cutting it off too early runs the risk of adult learners/staff doubting your intent and authenticity.

Demonstrate to adult learners/staff a clear intent to understand and, address the issues raised by reflecting comments, showing empathy, and discussing their concerns.

### *Authenticity is everything*

People know when you are being authentic. It is key that you are able to demonstrate your authenticity: over many years we have met people who are authentic but not demonstrative. The managers in the first two case studies demonstrated authenticity in terms of what they were trying to achieve, and how they interacted with their staff. The manager in the third case study is anything but authentic.

The importance of authenticity in successfully leading and developing teams cannot be emphasised enough. As French dramatist Jean Giraudoux (1882–1944) wrote: 'The secret of success is sincerity. Once you can fake that you've got it made'. While the authors agree with Giraudoux's first sentence, we strongly advise readers against attempting the second.

### *Clear objectives*

Leading teams, developing teams, and encouraging them to great performance requires that clear objectives are set. The first two case studies demonstrate this principle, and the first example in the third case study demonstrates the effect not doing this can have on adult learners/staff. One feature of objective setting in the first two case studies was that it was consensus-based. This may not be an appropriate approach to take in all circumstances, and your assessment of whether to adopt this approach or a more directive approach will depend on specific circumstances.

### *Be prepared to lead by example*

In the first case study, the manager was prepared to 'roll up his sleeves' to demonstrate the level of quality that was required. This also had the beneficial effect of demonstrating authenticity to the team where the manager was an unknown quantity to many of them. Leading by example also assists in providing the team with a consistent experience which helps morale – this consistency came through in the second case study. The third case study shows how not to lead by example! Micromanagement of adult learners/staff is often a good indicator of this: if you catch yourself micromanaging, remember that you are to lead by example only, not do the work for them!

### *Ask, don't tell*

The collaborative nature of the approaches in the first two case studies was a critical success factor in the great outcomes achieved. There is always a time for taking a direct approach, but where possible a collaborative approach where you seek input and incorporate that into the approach you are taking yields better outcomes and greater commitment from the team. This empowers people, and allows for full credit of ideas to be transparent across the team. It also allows for acknowledgement, both during the creation phase, and afterwards, or acknowledgements of team member efforts – in a peer setting.

This principle is tightly coupled with the second principle: it's difficult – if not impossible – to achieve an 'ask, don't tell' culture if people do not feel safe in sharing their feelings and ideas.

### *Understand and respect individual differences in your team*

The first case study showed through the example of the technical writer that the manager understood that not all team members had the same competencies and attributes. Likewise, the manager in the second case study understood that there were different roles in a hierarchical sense (scientists and technicians) and that an appropriate balance between the two was essential if the agreed objectives were to be achieved. Each person brings his/her own approach and skills to a team: these differences are to be celebrated and should be exploited (in a positive way) for meeting the team objectives.

### *Staff training and rewards*

Similar to the previous theme, how adult learners/staff expect to be rewarded differs enormously. The second case study showed the importance to some people of professional development over financial rewards; the third case study showed the impact ignoring staff development could have on people. The team in the first case study obtained reward through the achievement of something that was really cool, and, for most team members, the knowledge that successful completion of the project would make their regular jobs easier and more satisfying.

## Final thoughts

Please take the above suggestions as advice only, and do not treat them as a silver bullet. As an adult educator who is responsible for supervising, managing, coaching, mentoring or teaching you will need to think about your context, the make-up of your team, and how the team communicates in order to successfully apply these principles.

Finally, be prepared to listen to feedback from your team, from colleagues, and from mentors. The mark of a great manager is taking on board this feedback and appropriately changing one's behaviour. This will not only improve your own performance, but also the performance of your team. This includes being prepared to drop ideas that you may hold dear, and share control of decision making, as noted in CIO magazine: 'Top performers actively look for opportunities to make joint decisions and achieve them. The collaboration and influence competency is in part about engaging others, but it is also about giving up sole ownership of an idea or decision' (Lewke and Kelner, 2007, paragraph 3).

## Provocation

1. Am I being authentic? How aware am I of my own strengths and weaknesses? Am I demonstrating this authenticity?
2. Am I leading by example?
3. Have I set up an environment where staff can express how they feel without fear of repercussions? If not, what do I need to change in order to create that environment?
4. How clear are my objectives? Can I show the objectives to someone outside of my context and they still make sense? Have I enabled and supported my staff to achieve the objectives?

5. Am I making too many statements? Do I need to ask more questions?
6. How well do I know my team members? How long is it since I have spent time with each member individually to learn more about them?
7. What happens when we succeed? What changes? What are the tangible things that say, as a team, we have succeeded? Are these things important to the team members?

## References

Giraudoux, J. (undated). <https://en.wikiquote.org/wiki/Jean_Giraudoux>

Lewke, R. and Kelner, S. (2007). How good are you at collaboration and influence? *CIO Magazine,* 28 September 2007, retrieved from http://www.cio.com.au/article/194835/how_good_collaboration_influence_/ Accessed 31 October 2015.

Chapter 10

# Case studies in solution focused practice (SFP)

*Andrew Gibson and Greg Vinnicombe*

## Tribute

Sadly, while this book and chapter were in review, Greg Vinnicombe was killed in a road accident on 21 October, 2015. Greg dedicated his life to helping others and is greatly missed. He discovered Solution Focused Practice (SFP) nearly 20 years ago, and used it to great effect in supporting families in crisis, people with addictions, and many others with problems to solve. His study and practice of SFP led to him becoming a leader in the field, providing SFP training to many hundreds of people in many countries. He leaves a huge legacy of having made a difference, and his work is carried on by those who were privileged enough to have known him.

## Introduction

This chapter should help adult educators to become familiar with the basic principles and fundamental questions of Solution Focused Practice (SFP), which can be applied where progress is needed. As Berg and Miller (1992) indicated these are:

- If it ain't broke, don't fix it;
- If it works, do more of it;
- If it doesn't work, stop doing it.

This appears to be common sense. However, the key to effective SFP is to focus on the process and to stick to the model as it has been developed. Natural conversations such as seeking shared personal experience, or enquiring about feelings are not effective in helping the client to make their own progress. Useful conversations are structured around four questions. These are:

1. What do you want?
2. How will you know when you have it?
3. What are you doing already to get there?
4. What would be happening if you were a little closer to what you want?

(Iveson, 1999)

These principles and questions have been applied over the past 20 years to great effect in situations involving human interaction. They can be introduced to adult education in situations where progress needs to be made, for example where an adult learner is 'stuck'. Typical scenarios could be adult learners who are stuck in their studies, stuck with the learning options presented to them, or stuck considering the life choices they are making in the context of furthering their education.

For the teacher, coach or mentor, SFP is a valuable addition to other techniques employed to help others make progress. SFP is not intended to replace existing skills as it complements the set of skills that the adult educator brings to any learner interaction. SFP is an approach that benefits from study and practice.

Various solution focused practitioners will have slightly different and evolving perspectives on what constitutes SFP and how they apply this to their own area of work. For the purposes of this chapter we describe a typical SFP process they have implemented with their adult learners and which they consider to be a fair reflection of the SFP model.

## Solution Focused Practice (SFP)

Solution Focused Practice (SFP) begins by establishing and exploring the adult learner's goals. In simple terms how would the adult learner like things to be? Exploring this in some detail enables the adult educator to work out the differences that the adult learner is seeking upon achievement of the goal s/he has presented. This can open up options to achieve these differences, helping the adult learner to identify alternative ways of making progress.

Next, enquiring what parts of this description is happening already or has happened before, helps the adult learner identify both what is working already and what could easily happen again. Sometimes at this point it is enough for the adult learner to continue doing more of what s/he has already identified works well for her/him to make progress towards her/his goals, or more specifically, the differences that s/he seeks.

Further SFP questioning helps adult learners to establish the differences they would notice when they have made some progress towards their goals. This is an important step in practising SFP. Identifying these differences encourages adult learners to elaborate on the goals they seek, before considering some of the alternative things they and others can do to achieve some or all of these differences. Following this process, the original goal as presented will often be amended, or will change to something different altogether. The outcome of this process is to generate solutions that will deliver the differences that are sought by the adult learner.

As an adult educator you will note such an approach complements traditional teaching in many ways. Traditional teaching relies on the expert knowledge of the teacher and the willingness of the student to learn from this knowledge. SFP assumes that while the adult educator brings important professional knowledge, the adult learner has most or all of the knowledge and resources required within her/himself and her/his network to put the knowledge relevant to her/his circumstances into practice. Hence, SFP helps an adult learner to make decisions and progress on her/his own terms rather than those of the adult educator.

## Applying Solution Focused Practice (SFP)

As outlined above, Solution Focused Practice is based on a small number of elements. These are simple to understand, but not always so easy to practice.

For example, consider a parent trying to manage a toddler having a tantrum by asking the child to simply stop doing what s/he is doing, or unsuccessfully guessing what the toddler wants. This is mostly followed by the child becoming even more irate! Applying SF practice (after offering some reassurance) the parent would assist the child to identify what would help and what the child could possibly do instead (Lipchik, 2002).

As an adult educator you may have already determined that engaging with others in this way is not necessarily easy or simple to do. An effective SFP practitioner will be well versed in this questioning style of working with others. Developing all skills, commitment and practice increases confidence and ability.

For the purposes of providing context, we will now expand on the four SFP questions before illustrating their application in our adult learner case study.

### *1. What do you want?*

Returning to the above scenario, if you are a parent of a toddler, next time s/he is crying in frustration, try asking what s/he wants. You might not be able to give it to the child, but you will see the essential response that happens in people of any age. Usually, the toddler will stop crying (which is always good), think about the question (which is even better as s/he is distracted now), and the child may propose the thing that s/he wants. This (or a close alternative) might be easily given, and both parent and toddler can move on.

When working with adult development, the answer to this question is not often as easy as a chocolate button or a favourite toy. Often, when presenting a problem or seeking help to progress, the learner is told what s/he can have and then a negotiation is conducted to find something that fits within the provider's constraints.

Trusting the SFP model and finding out what the child or adult learner wants is the start of the SFP process and making progress. It is not an offer of full provision of their desired outcome, but it helps to get started.

### *2. How will you know when you have it?*

Exploring this aspect of the goal will provide context. The more detail that can be extracted, the more context is formed. This can include the resources that are available to adult learners, including the network of supporters that they can draw on for help if they need it. In addition to providing context, this identifies the differences that will be noticed if the desired outcome was achieved. By exploring what an adult learner would notice was different when s/he reaches her/his goal; the adult learner will start to understand the differences that s/he is looking for. Through this SFP process, many adult learners begin to realise that a lot of the differences they seek are attainable by other means, or may even be happening already.

### 3. What are you doing already to get there?

This is where you as an adult educator look into what is already working. This involves establishing the abilities and resources that adult learners and their networks are already drawing upon. It is very rare that an adult learner has nothing to contribute to this section of the conversation. Even if s/he states that things are the worst they have ever been you can usually elicit the managing or coping skills and resources utilised by the adult learner since the time that the problem was recognised. There may also have been times when her/his situation was better, or the problem that s/he faced happened less often, or even not at all. This gives you the opportunity to explore the interactional details of what was going well to contribute to this exception and to find more abilities and resources on which to build.

Spending time reflecting on the progress made and identifying strengths that are already making a positive contribution is a very positive part of the process. This creates hope and regularly reduces the 'size' of the problem from the learner's (and often the adult educator's) perspective. The adult learner will have invested time focusing on the problem and if this is done in isolation, the problem seems to be huge. By building the picture of the adult learner's abilities and resources, both her/his self-efficacy and the possibility of finding solutions increases.

### 4. What would be happening if you were a little closer to what you want?

Having explored what the adult learner wants, the differences s/he is seeking, and the abilities and resources s/he can build on, we now have the opportunity to explore what would be different if a small step was taken towards the desired future state. This often automatically leads to practical actions being identified by the adult learner that are within her/his capacity to implement, helping her/him to make progress. If this doesn't happen we would usually enquire 'What would it take for that to happen?' This helpfully prompts adult learners to describe possible alternatives they can work with before the next SFP session.

Finally, our experience over several years of applying SFP has demonstrated that by applying this process and spending as little time as possible on analysing the deficits to be overcome (the problems, barriers, things that are going wrong and not wanted), our adult learners usually start to make progress towards their desired outcomes and the deficits identified reduce in impact, and often disappear altogether.

## Using Solution Focused Practice (SFP)

As can be seen from following these steps, SFP builds confidence which in turn leads to capability and capacity enhancement. Subsequent SFP meetings include an exploration of what has gone well since the last meeting. Recognising adult learners' successes assists in developing their confidence in their abilities to influence their circumstances and encourages them to keep doing what has worked. Sometimes there is no need for further questioning in these sessions as the adult learner reports s/he will do more of what works, or starts describing what s/he will next do differently. Otherwise the structured conversation already presented can be utilised again.

We now move onto the case study to demonstrate SFP in action and to demonstrate the developmental journeys enjoyed by the participants, both practitioner and adult learner.

## Case study

### *Our client – background*

The client, Joe, was the manager of a charity that provided support for the families and friends of children affected by cancer. Joe initially explained that the charity was responsible for raising all of its funds through its large network of community and corporate supporters and from events and activities. These monies were then used in providing family support and funding medical research into childhood cancer. The Board of Trustees oversaw the workings of the charity and was striving to respond to the requirements of the charity's service users. As the manager, Joe provided regular guidance to the Board of Trustees regarding strategy and progress and oversaw the implementation of its decisions on a day-to-day basis. Joe had an established career in the charity sector, and had been appointed Charity Manager a few months before his first meeting with Andrew Gibson.

### *Case study stage 1.1 – Solution Focused Practice consultation*

One of the first challenges presented by Joe was a long list of changes that he would like to make. The perceived size of the challenge was overwhelming. He was not helped by a number of factors, some historical and some current. The six key issues he raised in our initial consultation were:

1. Our adult learner had numerous opportunities to support families affected by childhood cancer, and needed help to prioritise and implement these;
2. The charity had a long and successful history, and a healthy funding position which would enable them to deliver more support;

3. The charity funded medical research and numerous opportunities were presented for consideration;
4. The Board of Trustees was large as a result of a policy which was incorporated when the charity was founded, but which had not been reviewed;
5. In order to manage this unwieldy board, the current Chair took a keen interest in operational affairs;
6. The charity had limited numbers of people available to implement their activities, both in paid and voluntary capacities.

### *Case study stage 1.2 – Establishing goals – 'What do you want?'*

The points 1 to 6 above were a list of aspects that Joe wanted, and some that he did not want. The temptation is to ask about how this set of circumstances came about, or how Joe was feeling about the situation. From an SFP perspective neither of these approaches would be helpful to making quick progress. In line with Solution Focused Practice principles, Andrew quickly moved to establishing what Joe wanted instead.

The list of opportunities and strengths were established by exploring with Joe, 'So how do you want things to be?' This generated the following list of desired outcomes:

- More certainty about how to prioritise and implement the numerous ways to support families affected by childhood cancer.
- More staff to implement the charity's activities.
- A better way of effectively managing the demand for funding medical research.
- A Board of Trustees that is effective in its role.
- Joe to be left to manage the day-to-day operational affairs of the charity.

#### *Application to adult education*

This initial stage of establishing goals sets a framework for the conversation that builds on the positive strengths that the adult learner has already working for her/himself. Moving onto the challenges the adult learner is facing is much easier when placed in the context of what is going well. In all of the following, the adult educator is looking for detail and context, so liberal use of 'Anything else?' and 'What else?' in the context of differences such as 'What else will you notice?' and 'What will others notice?' will help here. Some of the lines of questioning include:

- If we had a successful session today, what would success look like for you?
- What are your goals from today's session? What are your goals for the longer term?

- What challenges are you facing just now? Having established a long list, ask 'Which of these would you like to discuss today?'

### Case study stage 1.3 – Establishing the differences achieving the goals will make

Andrew and Joe then identified the other people who would interact with the charity as changes were made. They went through the six key issue bullet points establishing what would be the benefits for Joe, the Board of Trustees and the families supported by the charity when this was achieved. The following SFP questions explore the differences that will be realised when the goals were achieved.

- What would you notice was different?
- What would others notice?
- Be specific, e.g. 'What would [stakeholder] notice?'

#### *Application to adult education*

By exploring the differences that will be noticed by the adult learner and others who are interacting with the adult learner, we start to build a picture of the changes that the adult learner is aiming for. As we will see later on, we can then look for other ways of achieving these differences than the original adult learner goals, and even look for ways in which some of these differences are happening now, or can be realised easily.

### Case study stage 1.4 – Establishing what is already present and working well

Andrew and Joe then went through the six key issue bullet points establishing what was already present and working well for each. Taking them in the order that they were presented, Joe came up with the following for each:

- lots of families were being helped and supported in many ways, and the charity regularly received very positive feedback about the help and support they provide;
- the funding position was healthy and the forecasts were that fundraising activities would be successful;
- with established projects and more in the pipeline, the charity could point to a track record of identifying and supporting medical research in their field;
- many of the Trustees were keen to be more involved, and all brought skills which were relevant and diverse;
- a sub-committee structure had already been used successfully for the financial aspects of administering the charity.

By working through this list in some detail, Joe and Andrew developed a set of opportunities that would help them to build the future desired state of the charity.

### *Application to adult education*

Exploring the strengths that the adult learner has already exhibited will help her/him to find ways of coping with the challenges s/he is presenting to the adult educator. Creating a list of the things that are working well also builds confidence, and helps the adult learner to realise that s/he often has the resources already that will help her/him to achieve her/his goal.

## *Case study stage 1.5 – Establishing the next steps*

Andrew then asked Joe, 'What would he notice was different if the charity was slightly closer to achieving each of these goals?' and finally 'What would that take?'

Following on from reviewing the list of what was going well, it was apparent that a method of delivering more of these activities was required. It was also clear that particular Trustees would be more helpful with certain activities. It was then possible to identify the likely contributors and supporters from the existing network of stakeholders. This saved a great deal of time and effort.

Andrew and Joe identified that the primary need was to deliver more of the successful current activity. They explored the various options that were open to Joe to make progress. This led to the idea of moving into larger premises adjacent to the local infirmary, and then using this space to employ more people in key operational and fundraising positions.

Having developed this goal, Joe and Andrew considered what would be possible if this was achieved, and what differences that would make. Joe's eyes lit up, and he came up with a long list, specifically including the following:

- the service provision to our families would be increased and improved;
- the services we offer would be spread to the whole county;
- more sustainable fundraising activities would be in place;
- we would be providing more and better support to our families;
- the funding for excellent medical research in the area of childhood cancer would be delivering real results.

Discussion of the differences made by achieving the goal unlocked the process of developing solutions that would improve family support. Andrew and Joe were then able to work together on plans to develop each strand individually. They also knew that they could work on these elements as they were within their control.

### *Application to adult education*

Working out the next small steps that an adult learner can take towards achieving her/his goal is a very helpful and useful conversation. This starts to develop a specific action plan so that the adult learner can quickly start making progress with manageable and achievable steps in the direction of her/his ultimate goal.

## *Case study stage 1.6 – How will you know when you have it?*

Key to identifying the changes needed is to work out the differences that will be noticed when these are achieved. The sub-committee structure was targeted at operational issues and the list of needs. Some of the questions used here included:

- Who is involved in this activity?
- What differences will they notice? (Be specific if there are a number of stakeholders and ask about each in turn.)
- What differences will you notice?
- What comments would you like to hear from [stakeholders] once you have realised your goal?

Using these questions generates detail about the reasons behind the activities listed and the differences these would make to people involved in and supported by the charity. Focusing on ways of delivering these differences opens up a breadth of possible solutions rather than focusing on delivering the one that was originally identified as the goal.

### *Application to adult education*

Exploring the differences that will be noticed by the adult learner and by her/his interactional network helps to identify more of the options open to the adult learner, as well as more of the sources of support s/he can draw on if help is needed. This may also help the adult learner to discover more of the things that are already happening and the comments people are already making that will give her/him confidence that s/he can achieve her/his desired outcomes.

## *Case study stage 1.7 – What are you doing already to get there?*

The charity was already providing services to families so there was a solid base on which to build. Also, funds were available to deliver the plans that were now in development. Each sub-committee member could look at what was already happening successfully in her/his area of responsibility, and then work from this base.

Questions to explore here are:

- What is working well?
- What comments would you like to hear from the people in your area?
- Are you getting any of these comments already?
- If you are getting these comments already, what is happening in that area that is already working?

These questions find details that can be transferred across areas of responsibility.

Once the goal of providing a physical space had been identified, work could then begin in earnest to find a suitable building in the best geographical area. SFP helped to identify the additional services that could be provided if more space was available, and this task was delegated to the Family Support sub-committee to research.

### *Application to adult education*

Sometimes, the adult learner will already have demonstrated the outcomes that s/he seeks, perhaps in whole, or in part. Looking for what is working well already, or has worked well in the past helps them to identify more small steps that s/he can take to help her/him progress.

## *Case study stage 1.8 – What would be happening if you were a little closer to what you want?*

The answer to this question provides the next small steps that can be taken in the direction of travel towards delivering the desired future state. In this section, the coach will focus on the differences that are desired and only then ask the adult learner what they and others could possibly do to make some of those differences happen. Having identified differences, some of these can often be realised very simply. In this case, Joe's answer was quite simple:

- the sub-committees would be developing plans in their areas of responsibility;
- these plans would be presented to the Board of Trustees for review and approval;
- once approved, the plans would be implemented by the operations team.

### *Application to the wider arena*

This final stage of the process develops the specific action plan. As you will have realised, there are many steps towards coming up with the action plan. All benefit the adult learner as they systematically identify strengths and resources, establish options and priorities, develop tangible next steps, and then finally create increased confidence that progress can be made through a specific set of small steps that are achievable now.

## *Case study stage 2 – Developing a Solution Focused Practice organisation*

Each meeting between coach and client consisted of the following simple structure:

- What has worked well since we last met?
- What progress has been made towards realising the differences we have identified?
- What are your next steps?
- What support do you need, and where will you find it?

This simple meeting format enabled Joe to make excellent progress.

By Joe sharing the differences sought with Trustees and colleagues, all aligned themselves behind Joe's delivery plans. Joe noted that by involving everyone in the discovery of solutions, the period of implementation was effective and efficient.

Most importantly, all of the ideas, plans, activities, proposals, resources and solutions had come from Joe and his colleagues, or from finding out what was working elsewhere already. Thus, although beginning with a long list of challenges presented by the client through helpful questioning from Andrew, the answers were all found within the capability of the client.

### *Application to the wider arena*

Where an adult learner is involved in regular review meetings with the adult educator, adopting a meeting format that uses SFP is a very helpful way of assisting the adult learner to focus on her/his strengths, and to recognise the progress s/he has made already before working on the next steps s/he wishes to make to further her/his studies.

## *Case study stage 3 – Solution Focused Practice culture*

We have outlined the first few months of what has been a two-year Solution Focused Practice (SFP) support programme. This successful beginning led to Greg and Andrew being engaged to deliver SFP training to all staff members in Solution Focused Practice so that they could apply SFP to their individual job roles. Feedback indicated this has been very effective in helping staff members when dealing with situations with service users, colleagues, Trustees and external parties.

## *Case study stage 4 – Solution Focused Practice help for families*

A further interesting development was not on the original project plan: the provision of SFP support for families. Solution Focused Practice is drawn from the assumptions and 'tools' developed in Solution Focused Practice Brief Therapy; a talking therapy used extensively to provide support in a number of clinical situations.

The development of our ideas resulted in the provision of SFP Brief Therapy as a service that is available in the new family support centre. This service was provided by Greg Vinnicombe. Greg provided a service called 'Open Discussions' that used SFP to help anyone affected by childhood cancer to keep going and to find ways forward. The process Greg used is very similar to that described above. Each open discussion asks questions to establish:

- what is wanted by those attending the sessions;
- what is 'the best that things can be' for those affected by the child's diagnosis of cancer;
- what is already happening that is contributing to how they would like things to be and how more of this can happen;
- any small steps that will help them make progress.

Early findings indicate that this gentle intervention through mostly three or less sessions is assisting clients in traumatic situations to find ways to keep going and to make progress in many aspects of their lives.

## Conclusion

As we hope has been demonstrated to the reader in this chapter, SFP as applied by Andrew Gibson and Greg Vinnicombe helped an individual to transform his organisation to undertake rapid growth in service provision, achieving his desired differences and furthering the organisation's aims and objectives. We believe SFP has much to offer adult teachers/mentors/supervisors/coaches in quickly and simply extending their repertoire of abilities to assist in the learning and development of others. Adult educators will have knowledge and skills that work for you and your students. In line with the principal of 'If it works, do more of it', we would encourage you to employ the tools that work in any given situation. SFP is an option that helps when the mentee/learner has become 'stuck' and needs help to make progress and to become unstuck. It is not intended to be a replacement model for existing practices.

The authors know that SFP can be applied to make a difference in many fields of human interaction including: personal coaching, organisational and business development and both individual and family support. It is also known that within teaching too, the fundamentals of this approach have already been applied with the growing popularity of concepts such as developing a 'Growth Mindset' (Dweck, nd) and through projects to increase student attendance and performance and to improve behaviour by reducing bullying.

Applying SFP, teachers, coaches, mentors and supervisors can begin by recognising that the adult mentee or learner (in this case Joe and his charity) is likely to hold much of the knowledge, skills and resources needed to implement effective change. By applying the SFP process and enabling adult mentees or learners to develop their own ways forward, this will show benefits for both the adult educator and the adult mentees or learners in terms of effective outcomes and in reducing the time spent and effort required to achieve these outcomes; something everyone will welcome.

## Provocation

To enable practical application, the principles and questions can be expanded as:

- look for what is working rather than at what is the problem and build on these strengths.
- consider, 'Is it possible to do more of what is working?' Can we look elsewhere to see if we can 'borrow' someone else's working idea/s and apply it to our own situation?
- don't worry about things that aren't working. Analysing and fixing the problem results in a well analysed and repaired problem; not necessarily a solution.

Then, asking some questions of your adult mentees or learners will help to establish the SFP structure for a useful conversation from their, and hopefully your, perspective:

- try to establish the goals for the adult mentees or learners and also for today's session;
- elicit what difference/s your adult mentees or learners (and others) will notice when they achieve their goals. Through this you may find alternative goals that will make the same (or better) difference if achieved;
- look at what is working, and see if that is helping us to achieve the differences we are looking for;
- and finally, consider what small steps learners and others can take, perhaps using resources that they already have, to make progress towards the differences they are looking for.

Following this simple process should lead to solutions and more importantly helps adult mentees or learners to make progress on their own terms. Another benefit is that progress is typically noticed very early in the intervention process, so adult mentees or learners quickly feel that their circumstances are improving. This builds confidence that in turn encourages more progress, and typically capacity is developed within the learner that will last beyond the SFP intervention.

## References

Berg, I. K. and Miller, S. D. (1992). *Working with the problem drinker: A solution-oriented approach.* New York: Norton.

Iveson, C. (1999). Presentation at BASW organised SF and Social Work Conference on 9 September 1999. (Developed from the original idea of Steve de Shazer.)

Lipchik, E. (2002). *Beyond technique in solution-focused therapy: Working with emotions and the therapeutic relationship*. New York: Guilford Press.

Dweck, C. (nd). Growth mindset. Retrieved from https://www.youtube.com/watch?v=QGvR_0mNpWM

## Chapter 11

# Promoting twenty-first century skills development among international adult learners

*Miia Rannikmäe, Jack Holbrook and Bulent Cavas*

## Introduction

It is clear from many studies that science educators and particularly teachers have not been able to reduce an alarming decline in students' interest in science, mathematics and technology (Potvin and Hasni, 2014). According to a report published by the European Commission (Rocard et al., 2007), the science education community mostly agrees that pedagogical practices based on inquiry-based methods are more effective for the teaching and learning of science. However, the reality of classroom practices in the majority of European countries is that inquiry-based methods are only being implemented by relatively few teachers.

In addressing these concerns, many novel approaches to science education attempt to revolutionise Science, Technology, Engineering, and Mathematics (STEM) education. These have led to attempts to interrelate science and technology to a real-world context, based on a context-based approach related to one of four orientations – a setting of focal events, a behavioural environment, use of specific language, extra-situational background knowledge (Gilbert et al., 2009). This promotes a more social and/or personal vision (Holbrook and Rannikmäe, 2007) in science related topics e.g. a focus of education towards 'education for all' as a democratic development as opposed to one of economic development for the country seen as promoting elitism and greater attention to those who are more gifted (Tytler, 2007).

## The issue

Europe and the whole world needs more educated people who have scientific competences to be able to function in the modern world and even more scientists (in the STEM sense) in order to meet challenges related to new developments in science, medicine, economic growth, security and policy directions (EC, 2004). More and more, it has been recognised that science education at school has narrowly focused on the subject content, building on conceptualisations from a past era and has become largely irrelevant in the eyes of the learners.

In this chapter, we introduce an approach and an associated model that can be used as a tool to help teachers to establish relevance of science education at all levels. Such relevance is defined from a learner's perspective, yet with a focus on a need to establish a base for lifelong learning, responsible citizenship and employability awareness, including a readiness to enter into the world of innovation and a recognition of responsible research.

We are well aware that, in general, people have little interest in topics that are perceived to be irrelevant to their lives, or career aspirations. However, it does not necessarily mean that which is relevant stimulates interest. Relevance and interest are only the beginning. To enhance a wider vision of the impact of science and technology, aptly referred to as enhancing scientific and technological literacy (Holbrook and Rannikmäe, 2007; 2009), there is a growing recognition of the need for self-development. This encompasses a proficiency in a range of cross-curricular skills, sometimes referred to as twenty-first century skills (NRC, 2010; Partnership for 21st Century Skills, 2009). Examples are often described as complex communication skills (communication in a variety of formats) and non-routine problem solving (systems thinking) as major considerations for science education development. Or to help students' achieve proficiency in twenty-first century skills, teachers need education support systems that strengthen their instructional leadership and management capacity (OECD, 2013).

Whereas science education in the twentieth century might be typically expressed as promoting the 'science of the scientists', with teachers focusing on promoting students as little scientists, a strong twenty-first century realisation is that science educators need to guide teachers to focus more widely on 'science for life', entrepreneurship in a democratic society and for acquiring workplace skills (Tytler, 2007). It is these skills and capacities to learn and to function in today's society, backed up by knowledge acquisition abilities, to which science education today needs to strive. For a move towards a more society-related approach, a more interdisciplinary approach is needed, related to the real world and the scientific literacy aspects of a systems approach, non-routine problem solving, adaptability and self-development related to this (NRC, 2010; Holbrook and Rannikmäe, 2007).

Holbrook and Rannikmäe (2007) suggest 'education through science' more appropriately reflects the intention of school science than science through education. As such, the term 'education through science' meaningfully captures the need to promote twenty first century skills as well as capturing the competences associated with conceptualising major scientific ideas.

## The three-stage model and its theoretical background

For an adult educator seeing science education wider than the content and skills of science promotes the concept of 'education through science' (as opposed to the more traditional 'science through education'). Thus science education focuses on enhancing multidimensional scientific and technological literacy for all students (Holbrook and Rannikmäe, 2007) rather than promoting 'apprentice scientists'. An associated teaching approach has attracted attention by advocating the teaching of science from a relevance perspective and hence recognising the need for learning to be context-driven. Relevance in the eyes of learners (Holbrook and Rannikmäe, 2009) can be tackled by relating the initial learning to a familiar issue or concern, which, for the most part, can be considered as socio-scientific. The goal is to enhance students' intrinsic motivation and promote the students' self-determination (Ryan and Deci, 2000). To enhance such learning, a three-stage model is put forward. It can be described as contextualisation (learning within a meaningful context), followed by de-contextualisation (learning in an unfamiliar context; in this case dominated by new learning within the subject), leading to re-contextualisation (the new subject–related learning is incorporated in a meaningful context) (Holbrook and Rannikmäe, 2010). This three stage model can be used to support adult education. Figure 11.1 elaborates the three different stages.

Stage 1– Contextualisation of the learning approach – promotes learner relevance by focusing on a societal issue and thereby arouse the student's intrinsic motivation. Where the context is relevant and motivational, it is expected to initiate discussion, drawing on the adult learner's background and thus providing an indicator of prior interdisciplinary science knowledge. Such an approach can also provide a stimulus for the need-to-know learning which follows and from this, the determination of a meaningful question which drives the subsequent inquiry-based, or problem-based learning. An adult educator is thus charged with identifying a motivational stimulus through a carefully derived scenario, purposely socio-scientific to relate to everyday life. In this manner, the context of the scenario is carefully chosen so that the scientific components are embedded and the actual conceptual science learning begins when these are decontextualised (Holbrook and Rannikmäe, 2010) from the initial context and an inquiry-based approach to the science learning is subsequently pursued.

Stage 2 – De-contextualisation – focusing on implementing scientific methods in the process of acquiring new knowledge and skills.

The second stage is thus science learning moving from a specified scientific question through the planning, investigatory and interpretation stages, as de-contextualised science learning, before being identified through well-formulated scientific problem solving and then consolidation of the conceptual science learning. An adult educator supports teachers by guiding them to focus on a structured, guided, or open inquiry style approach, all suitably scaffolded in line with meaningful challenges, focused within their zone of proximal development (Vygotsky, 1978). Also, science learning needs to go beyond inquiry-based learning and the problem-based solution to the scientific question posed. The conceptualised science needs to be consolidated and interrelated to prior conceptual learning, by for example using carefully constructed concept maps (Novak

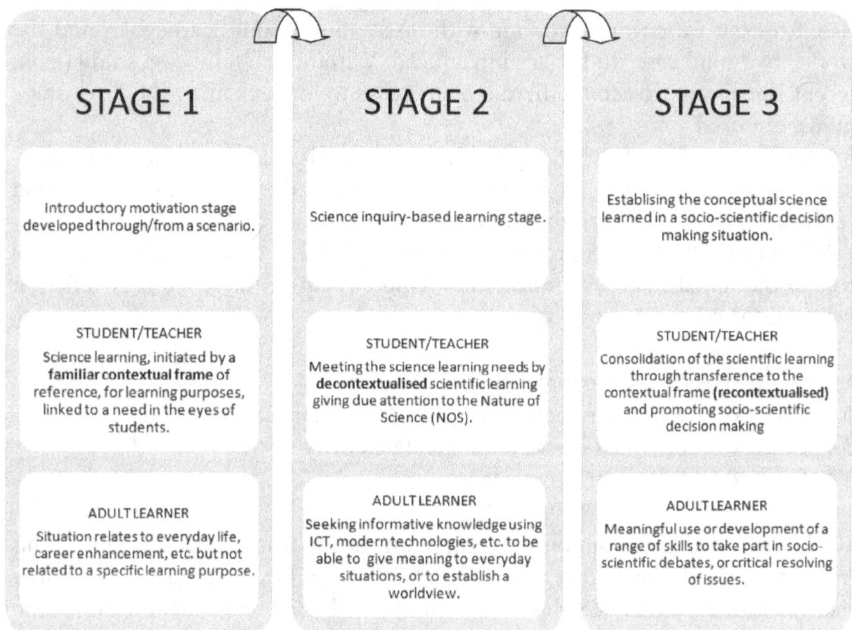


*Figure 11.1* The Education through Science approach using a three-stage model: contextualisation, de-contextualisation, re-contextualisation

and Gowin, 1984). But, the adult educator needs to ensure teachers recognise this is still not enough, as science learning is in a de-contextualised format and as such has not been related to the intended learning associated with everyday life in the real world.

For Stage 3 – Re-contextualisation – consolidation of the conceptual science is given relevance by including the science ideas in a socio-scientific scenario. A re-contextualised stage is thus needed, in which the adult educator needs to ensure teachers relate the science back to the initial concern or issue. The challenge an adult educator faces is to make teachers aware that the third stage is justified decision-making in a socio-scientific environment which takes note of real-life factors seen as relevant e.g. risk assessment, sustainable development, environmental issues, the economic factor, political considerations or an entrepreneurial approach and not forgetting ethical and moral aspects.

Figure 11.1 illustrates the three-stage model from a student/teacher and adult learner perspective. For such a model, there is no suggestion that time allocation is equal at each stage. Nor is there any suggestion that the adult educator tells the teacher to focus on only certain conceptual areas from studying any one scenario. But there is a requirement that the teacher facilitates the learning in relation to the real world of the learner.

## Illustrative case studies

Based on our experiences working with international adult learners around the world, two mini case studies are introduced. Within each mini case study (from recent European projects), different approaches to implementing the three-stage model are used.

*Mini case study 1* – In-service provision for secondary science education – overcoming/ bridging the gap between different paradigms of science teaching (drawing on the European project PROFILES).

Within the PROFILES project (Bolte et al., 2012), context plays an essential role in the initial stage. As indicated by Gilbert (2006), there are four different orientations related to context:

1. Context as the direct application of concepts
2. Context as reciprocity between concepts and applications
3. Context as provided by personal mental activity
4. Context as the social circumstances.

While the first is the common standing point for the teaching of science and this may interact with the second context, the last two contexts are particularly essential within the PROFILES three-stage model and need to be identifiable within teaching–learning modules, both being based on activity theory (Engstrom, 2000) and situated learning (Lave and Wagner, 1990).

A case study carried out among Estonian teachers (Holbrook et al., 2014) showed that it was not so easy to understand and accept the philosophy and approach. From 31 science teachers, who attended a continuous or longitudinal in-service programme throughout one academic year, most highlighted the role of the initial scenario and its relevance for the learners. For successful teaching adult educators need to guide teachers to pay attention to:

- how the teaching module is introduced and the manner in which students are involved at the initial stage;
- how transfer from the initial stage to the second science inquiry stage is carried out;
- whether students were involved in the inquiry-based science education (IBSE) stage and the manner in which the IBSE stage is conducted;
- whether students are guided to consolidate/present their science conceptual learning, and
- whether science gained is used in a society setting to promote argumentation skills and socio-scientific decision making.

For teachers teaching at the secondary level, the idea of developing concept maps with their students, related to the motivational scenarios, was introduced and considerations explored on how to move from concept maps towards a flowchart. By constructing maps in collaborative settings, participants / learners share ideas as in real-life situations, gain mutual learning of science content and, in addition, social skills are embedded into the consequence maps.

Mini case study 1 highlighted the need for a motivational scenario in the form of 'cosmetics'. For adult educators, the key aspect was that they could guide teachers to identify a familiar setting as a base for the learning of the science and be able to introduce this in a socio-scientific manner.

In Stage 2, students are involved in inquiry-based learning in which they are asked to develop a range of sub-aspects, depending on the type of inquiry involved. As the ultimate target, students can undertake open inquiry, whereby the students provide all sub-aspects in the inquiry-based learning process.

For Stage 3, the major emphasis is on the consolidation of the science conceptual learning and the re-contextualisation of the science into a social frame. In so doing, the development of twenty-first century skills is promoted, especially the skill of argumentation using conceptually correct science and reasoning.

*Mini case study 2* – In-service provision at the primary and lower secondary education levels (drawing on the European project ENGINEER).

The case study involved teachers and the use of technology and robotics in the process of modelling everyday related problems. The main aim of this case study was to introduce engineering as a practical and career related use of scientific ideas and present experiences from an adult teaching and learning environment, which was conducted in Turkey.

Before embarking on the main aim of the workshop, which was geared to the professional development of teachers and introducing the use of engineering ideas in their teaching of science, the teacher participants were introduced to a wider vision of science education. In guiding the teachers to reflect on student relevant approaches, attention was given to the role of technology in scientifically related situations. This led to a consideration of who is a 'scientist' and sought to introduce engineering as a possible career choice and hence consideration of the role of an engineer.

As inquiry-based learning was a key focus for the professional development course, the teachers were also asked to reflect on the meaning of inquiry learning. This session included the idea of a 'Raising Questions' component, designed to help participants to see how this supports students in developing the skill of questioning.

After these introductory activities promoting relevance and inquiry learning, the teaching approach to science learning became the focus. This provided the opportunity to incorporate relevance and inquiry learning by means of a three-stage model. Here, participants were introduced to a teaching unit in which Stage 1 was a scenario describing a group of students asked to clear up after having held a party the previous evening The participants were introduced to a teaching-learning module, called 'Suck it up: Designing a contraption that sucks up debris'. The initial teaching approach was based on a social aspect, which was put into an appropriate socio-scientific context by means of a 'scenario' – a story, a situation, an elaboration of the title or other such triggers to initiate discussion. Interestingly, when the students were then asked, as part of the initial Stage 1, to explain the operation of vacuum cleaners that they used in their houses, the teachers, as expected, soon realised that the students lacked science understanding, which was important for a more in-depth discussion on the manner in which a vacuum cleaner can be developed and used. This realisation formed the basis for exploring within Stage 2 in the module. In the workshop, students were subsequently asked to design and create their own small vacuum cleaner. Stage 2 was an inquiry learning activity session. The science learning had a specific purpose – enabling the development of a useful product deemed appropriate to solve the problem faced.

In Stage 2 the approach guides teachers towards guided or open-inquiry style learning and maximising student involvement in the learning process. The extent to which scientific ideas are explored, or scientific problems are solved, depends on the scientific learning deemed necessary for an appreciation of the socio-scientific issues introduced in Stage 1. Stage 2 is, in substance, purely scientific (it is de-contextualised), although development of educational skills, such as, cooperative learning, scientific communication, and the development of perseverance, initiation, ingenuity, or safe working, are also intended.

Stage 3 is perhaps the most important. Here, the teachers consolidate their science learning by transferring the learning to the socio-scientific issue introduced in Stage 1 and, though discussion and reasoning, arrive at a socio-scientific decision. In this process, the actual decision made is of less importance than the reasoning put forward, and the degree to which the scientific component is included in a conceptually correct manner. This stage involves argumentation skills, leadership skills, the ability to reason using sound science ideas, and balancing these against other considerations, such as ethical, environmental, social, political and, of course, financial (Holbrook, 2008). In the last part of Stage 3, teachers compared their vacuum cleaners (reflecting on design, energy efficiency, noise etc.), discussed the efficiency of the vacuum cleaners and selected the best one to use and to develop further.

This case study seeks to show that the inclusion of career-related components, such as engineering design, can be a feature of the three-stage model (Figure 11.1). For the adult educator, relevance can stimulate motivation to learn. The subdivision of an inquiry-based approach enables a breakdown of a problem scientifically and through such steps as recognising the problem, planning for a solution and interpreting outcomes. This enables an adult learner to be better prepared to handle socio-scientific situations within the home, everyday life or related to employability.

## Provocation

The following are stimulus suggestions to help an adult educator working towards establishing a meaningful understanding of responsible research and innovation.

- How would you describe or identify relevance when applied to an adult learner – is this an aspect of everyday life or a construct for learning?
- How would you as an adult educator strive to involve others in tackling a socio-scientific issue?
- How would you as an adult educator use the three-stage model as a frame to help you with your adult learners?

## References

Bolte, C., Holbrook, J. and Rauch, F. (eds) (2012). *Inquiry-based science education in Europe: Reflections from the PROFILES Project.* Berlin: Freie Universität Berlin. Retrieved November 4, 2015, from http://techcrunch.com http://www.profiles-project.eu

European Commission (EC) (2004). *Europe needs more scientists.* Brussels: European Commission.

ENGINEER project (2014). Retrieved November 4, 2015, from www.engineer-project.eu

Engstrom, Y. (2000). Activity theory as a framework for analyzing and redesigning work. *Ergonomics*, 43(7), 960–974.

Gilbert, J. K. (2006). On the nature of 'context' in chemical education. *International Journal of Science Education*, 28(9), 957–976.

Gilbert. J. K., Bulte, A. M. W. and Pilot A. (2011). Concept development and transfer in context-based science education. *International Journal of Science Education*, 33(6), 817–837.

Holbrook, J. (2008). Editorial. In: Special issue on the PARSEL project, UK: ICASE Retrieved November 4, 2015, from: www.icaseonline.net/seiweb

Holbrook, J. and Rannikmäe, M. (2007). Nature of science education for enhancing scientific literacy. *International Journal of Science Education*, 29(11), 1347–1362.

Holbrook, J. and Rannikmäe, M. (2009). The meaning of scientific literacy. *International Journal of Environmental & Science Education*, 4(3), 275–288.

Holbrook, J. and Rannikmäe, M. (2010). Contextualisation, de-contextualisation, re-contextualisation – a science teaching approach to enhance meaningful learning for scientific literacy. In: I. Eilk and B. Ralle (eds), *Contemporary science education* (pp. 69–82). Aachen, Germany: Shaker Verlag.

Holbrook, J., Rannikmäe, M. and Valdmann, A. (2014). Identifying teacher needs for promoting education through science as a paradigm shift in science education. *Science Education International*, 25(2), 133–171.

Lave, J. and Wenger, E. (1990). *Situated learning: Legitimate peripheral participation.* Cambridge: Cambridge University Press.

National Research Council (NRC) (2010). *Exploring the intersection of science education and 21st century skills: A workshop summary.* Margaret Hilton, Rapporteur. Board on Science Education, Center for Education, Division of Behavioral and Social Sciences and Education. Washington, DC: The National Academies Press. Retrieved November 4, 2015 from www.nap.edu/catalog/12771.html

Novak, J. D. and Gowin, D. B. (1984). *Learning how to learn.* New York: Cambridge University Press.

OECD (2013). OECD skills outlook 2013: First results from the survey of adult skills, OECD Publishing. http://dx.doi.org/10.1787/9789264204256-en

Partnership for 21st Century Skills (2009). Framework for 21st century learning. Retrieved November 4, 2015, from www.p21.org

Potvin, P. and Hasni, A. (2014). Interest, motivation and attitude towards science and technology at K-12 levels: A systematic review of 12 years of educational research. *Studies in Science Education*, 50(1) 85–129. http://dx.doi.org/10.1080/03057267.2014.881626

Rocard, M., Csermely, P., Jorde, D., Lenzen, D., Henriksson, H. W. and Hemmo, V. (2007). *Science education now: A new pedagogy for the future of Europe*. European Commission Directorate General for Research Information and Communication Unit. Retrieved 15 February 2012, from http://ec.europa.eu/research/science-society/document_library/pdf_06/report-rocard-on-science-education_en.pdf

Ryan, R. M. and Deci, E. L. (2000). Self-determination theory and the facilitation of intrinsic motivation, social development and well-being. *American Psychologist*, 55, 68–78.

Tytler, R. (2007). Re-imagining science education. Engaging students in science for Australia's future. *Australian Education Review*, Camberwell, Vic. Australia: ACER Press.

Vygotsky, L. (1978). Problems of method. In: M. Cole (trans.). *Mind in society*. Cambridge, MA: Harvard.

Chapter 12

# Adult educators working with adult learners

## Applying theory and practice

*Heather Fehring*

### Introduction

In the world of adult education, which involves high speed and complex technological communication software there is sometimes a sense of the loss of the identity of the individual adult learner. The creation of rich vibrant learning environments is the goal for adult educators.

The challenge for adult educators is to design and deliver high-quality programmes that encompass a blend of teaching and learning approaches and strategies, that are constructed for adult learners in multiple educational environments, and that cater for the diversity of adult learners' needs. As the chapters in this book demonstrate, adult learners are complex individuals who come to the learning process with a multitude of different experiences. Many are working full-time jobs, many have family commitments that they need to juggle with their learning commitments, some have experienced failure in previous learning endeavours, some are coming to the adult learning environment as EAL (English as an Additional Language) learners, some come with visual impairments, some are undertaking a formal qualification to enhance their career opportunities (such as pre-service teachers and medical students) and some are participating in on-the-job professional development programmes. All have different learning needs that require accommodation to maximise their learning potential. There are many important issues to take into consideration when designing learning environments and learning materials to meet the needs of this diverse group of learners. Figure 12.1 illustrates an action research model that can form the basis of an adult educator's delivery programme.

To be able to target teaching to meet the needs of adult learners (also referred to as differential teaching), adult educators need to use evidence-based techniques (Griffin, 2014; Hattie, 2009, 2012). Educators need to evaluate the effectiveness of the programmes implemented, and they need to reflect on these data and then adapt or adjust their delivery practices accordingly. Finally, adult educators need to re-assess to verify the learners' achievement.

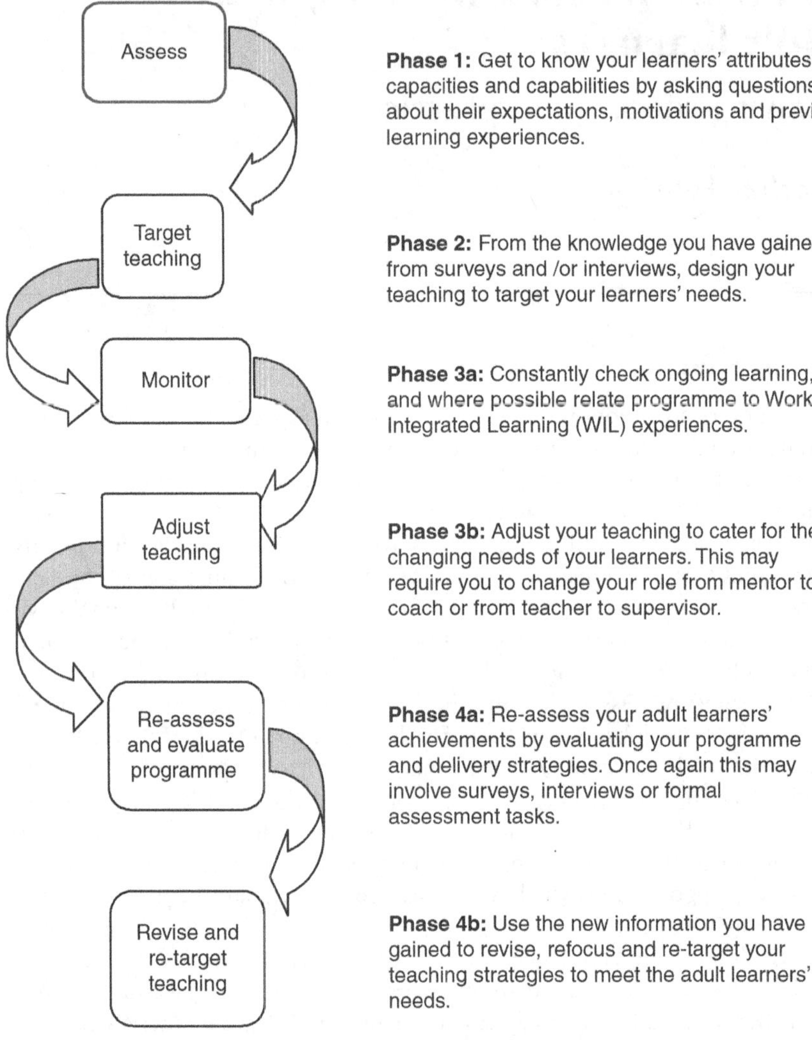


*Figure 12.1* Action research model for the delivery of adult learning

## Getting to know the learner and understanding the learning process

To create a positive learning environment, you, as an adult educator, need to take the time to learn about the attributes and capabilities of the adult learners who have come to learn. You should be asking questions such as: What are the expectations of the adult learners in the programme you are going to deliver? Why did the adult learners choose the programme on offer? Where did the adult learners come from in terms of previous education? What is the cultural background of the adult learners and how does this affect their potential? To commence the process, adult educators should undertake some preliminary assessment of the adult learners' capabilities, attributes, and access to and competence in the use of technology: as shown in Phase 1 of the Action Research Model for the Delivery of Adult Learning (Figure 12.1). You can undertake this assessment process before a programme commences by sending short surveys to programme participants using resources such as Survey Monkey or Qualtrics. By using online questionnaires, you can quickly gather demographic, educational and English proficiency information that can inform the design of the programme to be delivered. Face-to-face interviews can be tailored to collect personal information that programme participants may not feel comfortable providing in an online survey. Small group discussions and peer-sharing sessions at the beginning of a programme can not only provide an adult learner with invaluable data about what attributes a learner brings to the programme but also help build confidence and establish networks between adult learners. Asking the participants in your programme what their motivations are for undertaking the course and enquiring about the cultural and life experiences they bring to the programme are important questions. This knowledge will facilitate an adult educator to provide inclusive programmes that are structured for all learners.

Chapter 5 by Owen Barden, William Youl and Eva Youl discusses assessment strategies for an adult educator to use to assess relevant cultural differences of adult learners to deliver inclusive educational activities. In Chapter 6, Celia McDonald and Susan Rodrigues highlight the necessity of understanding the needs of visually impaired learners in any learning situation. They have provided very useful assessment questions to assist the adult educator when making decisions about how to deliver a programme involving visually impaired participants. Chapter 9 by Paul Edwards, Brian Rock and Elizabeth Gibson provides additional insights into how managers in industry, as adult educators, can assess their teams' capabilities when leading and developing teams of workers. They raise pertinent questions: What is the position of the team member in the organisational structure? What is the situational context to be dealt with such as regulatory constraints? What is the team member's opinion in relation to the task to be achieved?

In Chapter 1, Rita Ellul and Heather Fehring discuss how adult educators need to decide whether the teaching role will encompass a mentoring, coaching or supervising approach, or a blend of approaches (Darling-Hammond and McLaughlin, 1995; Jensen et al., 2014; OECD, 2009). Knowing if your role in the learning process is as an expert, a facilitator or a colleague influences the content to be delivered as well as the relationship that is established between adult educators and adult learners. As a mentor, you will be taking the role of an expert guiding a novice. However, the novice could be an early-career teacher or an experienced professional taking on a new senior management role. In both situations, as an adult educator, you will be facilitating the upskilling of the mentees to undertake the new expectations in their jobs. You will be using teaching strategies that involve encouraging learners to share and discuss their ideas and needs, providing supporting professional literature, modelling teaching practices or demonstrating and using team teaching strategies. As a coach, or more specifically a peer-coach, you will be taking on the role of a collegiate advisor structuring opportunities to enhance mutually supportive learning environments. You may be working on an identified learning need to adopt a new computer system in an industry or school administration context. You may start by ascertaining the level of knowledge of the computer system to be implemented to determine if the system will meet the needs of the operators. The adult educator needs skills in listening, and developing trust so that challenging prior knowledge is done in a supportive and productive manner, and experiences can be provided that allow trial and error in a positive learning environment. In both these scenarios, the adult educator will be assessing the learners' needs, adapting targeted teaching and learning strategies to meet the perceived needs of the learners, and constantly monitoring the situation to refine the delivery of the programme.

In Chapter 3, Carolina Guzmán-Valenzuela and Valeria Cabello point out that becoming a reflective learner is an empowering process for adults. However, it is not a process that occurs by osmosis, and adult learners need to be immersed in reflective practice learning environments and encouraged to develop these skills. Once again, early assessment of the needs of the learner and then targeted teaching practices to enhance the skills of reflective learning are integral parts of the process. Chapter 8 by Christine Redman and Deborah James highlights the need for adult educators to develop the professional resilience and professional learning of adult learners by developing their knowledge, skills and positive outcomes through relevant, authentic and meaningful experiences. Positioning and re-positioning adult learners in new ways of knowing requires skilful practitioners working in collegiate relationships. Christine and Deborah provide practical activities to foster adult learning engagement. These practical activities involve adult learners developing new practices, refining existing modes of operation, and adopting and adapting alternative ways of knowing and change. This, in turn, involves the adult educator assessing and targeting practices to meet the needs of the adult learners and then monitoring the progress of the learners. The use of challenging questions (e.g. How will you model the use of conflict in the learning context to increase appreciation in the participants of others' perspectives?) are proposed in their chapter to demonstrate how to achieve new knowledge.

In Chapter 4, Carl Gibson, Richard Holme and Neil Taylor remind us of the importance of understanding the learning process. They describe in detail how the brain functions and the traditional view of the transmission of information during the learning process. Although in-depth knowledge of the neuroscience and neuropsychology of the brain is not necessary, an understanding of how memory works and what affects knowledge retention is important for adult educators. Designing learning experiences to maximise the processing of complex conceptual knowledge and then transform the knowledge to new learning environments is fundamental to all learners. Therefore, the adult educator needs to have a working knowledge of the following:

- attention getting mechanisms;
- how to limit tasks to maximise learning;
- how much practice is beneficial and how much practice is repetitive and boring thus reducing learner engagement;
- the balance between subject-specific knowledge and problem-solving applied learning activities to form the building blocks of understanding;
- whether extrinsic or intrinsic motivational factors drives the learner;
- the balance of diet and physical exercise required to maintain active learning engagement;
- the impact of too much stress on the learning capacity of the individual.

All these considerations point to the need for adult educators to be lifelong learners in their understanding of the learning process. Continuing to keep in touch with advances in understanding the human mind will enhance adult educators' insights and capacities to design and deliver high-quality learning experiences for adult learners. Chapter 4 by Carl Gibson, Richard Holme and Neil Taylor's provides very helpful suggestions for both educator and student strategies that adult educators can take into consideration and incorporate into their programmes to target effective teaching and learning practices.

## Knowing the learning environment

Phase 2 of the Action Research Model for the Delivery of Adult Learning (Figure 12.1) requires adult educators to develop a targeted teaching and learning programme. This involves integrating information gained from Phase 1 and incorporating this knowledge about the learning environment in which both the educator and the learner will be situated to develop a targeted teaching and learning programme. Adult educators may be delivering programmes in a multitude of locations and for a multitude of different purposes. Some educators are involved in Transnational Educational (TNE) programmes. Educational programmes are often designed in one cultural context, such as Western countries, but delivered in another cultural context, for example, transnational educational programmes in China and Vietnam. Some adult learners may be undertaking informal short courses and others may be undertaking formal qualifications such as Certificates, Diplomas, Bachelors' degrees, Honours' degrees, Masters' degrees and Doctoral degrees. The demands of each programme will vary according to the academic requirements, including in some cases the professional registration requirements of the programme, and also to the personal and social needs of the individual. However, every learning environment needs to take into consideration the socio-cultural context of the adult learners. Adult educators need to familiarise themselves with knowledge of the cultural contexts influencing adult learners' engagement and interaction with the learning process. This knowledge is essential when designing a programme of learning that will be effective and efficient.

In Chapter 5, Owen Barden, William Youl and Eva Youl provide valuable examples of strategies to support the principles underpinning the importance of the cultural aspects of inclusive education. Inclusive education is a broad concept encompassing cultural diversity as well as disability needs. Understanding that the motivations of adult learners to undertake higher education programmes may include furthering career prospects, increasing salaries or changing career paths is important to know when structuring a programme. This knowledge facilitates an adult educators' selection of Work Integrated Learning (WIL) experiences, visits to industry locations, visits by practitioners to speak to the class and access to opportunities to experience work-based knowledge as well as subject-based knowledge. Acknowledging the English as an Additional Language (EAL) status of adult learners can be the first step in providing inclusive programme content. An adult educator can structure small group in-class interactions to provide opportunities for adult learners to speak in English or their first language. Owen, William and Eva have provided a very useful checklist to assist adult educators to ascertain the impact of the diverse cultural backgrounds of the participants in any adult learning programme.

In Chapter 11, Miia Rannikmäe, Jack Holbrook and Bulent Cavas further expands the reader's repertoire of strategies that can be incorporated into the design and planning of programmes for adult learners in their *three-stage model of learning through science*. Their work is related to the importance of acknowledging that learners need to understand the meta-language or discipline-specific literacy of science, that is, 'A disciplinary literacy approach emphasises the specialised knowledge and abilities possessed by those who create, communicate, and use knowledge within each of the disciplines' (Shanahan and Shanahan, 2012, p. 7). Disciplinary literacies are not just about looking at the similarities between the knowledge and abilities of disciplines but are also about highlighting the differences. This is important because research has shown that disciplinary literacies are closely connected to disciplinary achievement. In Chapter 11, Miia, Jack and Bulent provide strategies that adult educators can apply when constructing programmes for adult learners. Their chapter illustrates that through using problem-based inquiry learning approaches, adult educators involve adult learners in the creation of science-based learning concepts, cooperative learning skills, scientific communication leadership skills and scientific reasoning abilities. All these skills are fundamental to developing Science, Technology, Engineering and Mathematics (STEM) courses in the twenty-first century.

Chapter 10, by Andrew Gibson and Greg Vinnicombe, introduces yet another strategy for adult educators to use when designing and planning programmes for adult learners. Their Solution Focused Practice (SFP) strategy incorporates numerous examples of how to ascertain an adult learner's needs and how to plan successful programmes to work towards change.

## Monitor and adjust programme delivery

Phases 3a and 3b of the Action Research Model for the Delivery of Adult Learning (Figure 12.1) highlight the importance of ongoing monitoring, especially in relation to the notion of work-integrated learning and the impact on the learners. In addition, Phase 3 emphasises the importance of adjusting the learning environment to re-target the teaching and learning being delivered, when and where necessary. Chapter 9, by Paul Edwards, Brian Rock and Elizabeth Gibson, provides a wealth of strategies to facilitate this ongoing process in relation to managers' approaches to leading team workers to achieve organisational goals. The strategies documented include:

- tapping into team members' concerns, allowing them to 'vent', as the authors put it;
- asking rather than demanding compliance being a more inclusive strategy to obtain the desired results;
- alternating between giving explicit instructions and allowing team member autonomy creates a more productive working environment;
- involving staff members in objective setting because it enhances commitment to meeting goals;
- providing clear and regular communication practices being essential in the development of team building;
- positively communicating team members' performance objectives and benchmarking successes enhances team morale and staff retention.

Chapter 10 by Andrew Gibson and Greg Vinnicombe outlines the Solution Focused Practice (SFP) strategy and provides valuable sets of questions for an adult educator to ask adult learners undertaking a specific programme that enables the educator to monitor the learners' progress and then adapt the programme accordingly. Involving adult learners in self-reflection and monitoring of their own progress provides confidence, and develops capabilities.

## Evaluating and re-assessing to re-target the teaching programme

Evaluating all aspects of programme delivery involves not only re-assessing the learners' achievements but also the adult educators' own professional development needs. These processes are included in Phase 4 of the Action Research Model for the Delivery of Adult Learning (Figure 12.1). To be able to re-assess, refocus and re-target the teaching and learning activities you are providing as an adult educator is an essential part of programme delivery. In Chapter 4, Carl Gibson, Richard Holme and Neil Taylor highlight a number of the professional development needs of adult educators. They address the behavioural (pedagogical practices), attitudinal (perceptions, beliefs and values) and intellectual (practitioner knowledge) needs that pertain to the professional development of adult educators. First, as an adult educator, you may need to be an expert in your field. Secondly, you may also need to comply with statutory requirements in relation to professional qualifications and mandatory accreditation regulations, such as the standards of many professional associations. It is the responsibility of adult educators to be knowledgeable about the professional standards that apply to their occupation. It is also the responsibility of adult educators to evaluate themselves and assess their own professional development needs to deliver high-quality programmes. Linda Darling-Hammond (2011) in the Unites States and Stephen Dinham (Dinham, 2011; Dinham et al., 2008) in Australia both write frequently about the attributes of high-quality teaching and effective professional development. This is not an arduous process, but it does involve commitment and positive engagement with professional organisations that deliver professional development programmes to up-skill adult educators. Information technology advances mean that a myriad of opportunities are now available for obtaining access to formal and informal professional development programmes at any time and in any place. Knowing your own needs as an adult educator is important, and seeking opportunities to improve your own capabilities is essential as it affects the successful delivery of your programme.

In Chapter 2, Carey Normand and Maureen Morriss approach the professional development needs of adult educators from the perspective of professional identity. They highlight the need for adult educators to establish credibility through their expert knowledge in their chosen field of endeavour, as well as confidence and commitment to their profession. They acknowledge that adult educators may be working with adult learners in a higher education environment leading to a formal qualification. At other times, adult educators may be taking the role of consultants to organisations and institutions. In both cases, adult educators need to evaluate their programmes and re-assess their target teaching approaches often from an expert–novice perspective. Maintaining a professional identity as an adult educator can be enhanced by:

- developing an understanding of your own motivation as adult educators;
- projecting an enthusiastic attitude to the programme and the learners you are working with to produce a positive effect on the learner's engagement;
- becoming involved with other experienced adult educators to learn new practices;
- organising collegiate partnerships to share ideas and resources at a personal level and to facilitate your reflective capabilities;
- projecting an image of an adult educator who involves themselves at the grass roots level and who is a team player;

- developing high-level communication skills involving knowledge of body language effects, the necessity of a balance of speaking and listening to an audience, and the importance of punctuality on the establishment of your professional identity;
- maintaining an online portfolio to enhance your professional identity in the public arena.

Many of these professional identity attributes can be enhanced by attending informal seminars and workshops and by belonging to professional associations that publish journals or organise conferences where you can develop networks with other like-minded participants. In addition to reflecting on your own skills as an adult educator, there is a need to be constantly evaluating the programme you are delivering to ascertain if it meets the needs of adult learners.

In Chapter 7, Susie Schofield, Madawa Chandratilake and Hiroshi Nishigori provide an insightful analysis of how they assessed the use of technology in the supervision and teaching of medical education. By incorporating technology designed to enhance learning, learning about the technology used in the workplace and professionalism issues related to technology, this chapter highlights the many ways adult educators can evaluate teaching and learning programmes for adult learners. Susie, Madawa and Horoshi outline a number of possibilities to evaluate the effectiveness and efficiency of delivering curriculum content that is both relevant and engaging for medical students. This includes increasing the access to high-quality material, not only to distant education learners, but also 24/7 access to all adult learners. Their chapter describes costs, availability and how to use the following as teaching and learning tools and evaluation tools:

- Flipped classrooms (viewing lectures online so that face-to-face time can maximise more active interaction).
- PowerPoint and/or Prezi presentations (visual learning environments – VLE).
- Technology-enhanced simulation training using YouTube videos, Moodle, Webinars and Web-Ex.
- Global communication strategies, (e.g. Skype and mobile devices).
- Work Integrated Learning fundamentals in clinical settings.

Susie, Madawa and Hiroshi also raise the very pertinent issues of integrity and ethical considerations that need to be addressed when using confidential client information. Transferring patients' private details and data on the Internet and e-learning systems of social network communication can be fraught with privacy infringement issues. Being aware of copyright and patent issues when using material obtained from the Internet is another complex consideration for students. Although raised in the context of medical education, ethical considerations related to the use and transfer of information are very relevant to pre-service teachers and, indeed, all adult learner environments.

All the chapters in this book bring together a wealth of ideas, suggestions, strategies and case studies to assist the adult educator when designing and implementing programmes for adult learners. By using the Action Research Model for the Delivery of Adult Learning (Figure 12.1) and the many recommendations in this book, an adult educator can enhance the learning of all adult learners.

## References

Darling-Hammond, L. (2011). *The flat world and education. How America's commitment to equity will determine our future.* Moorabbin, Victoria: Hawker Brownlow Education.

Darling-Hammond, L. and McLaughlin, M. W. (1995). Policies that support professional development in an era of reform. *Phi Delta Kappan*, 76(8), 597–604.

Dinham, S. (2011). Let's get serious about teacher quality: The need for a new career architecture for Australia's teachers. The University of Melbourne Dean's Lecture 27 September 2011. Retrieved 28th September, 2011, from http://www.edfac.unimelb.edu.au/news/lectures/pdf/S%20Dinham%20PowerPoint%2027.9.11.pdf

Dinham, S., Ingvarson, L. and Kleinhenz, E. (2008). Teaching talent. The best teachers for Australian classrooms. Paper prepared for The Business Council of Australia. Retrieved 14th September, 2011, from http://www.bca.com.au/Content/101446.aspx

Griffin, P. (ed.) (2014). *Assessment for teaching.* Port Melbourne, Victoria: Cambridge University Press.

Hattie, J. (2009). *Visible learning: A synthesis of over 800 meta-analyses relating to achievement.* London: Routledge.

Hattie, J. (2012). *Visible learning for teachers: Maximizing impact on learning.* London: Routledge.

Jensen, B., Hunter, J., Sonnemann, J. and Cooper, S. (2014). Making time for great teaching. Grattan Institute Report. Retrieved Report No. 2014-3, from http://grattan.edu.au/wp-content/uploads/2014/03/808-making-time-for-great-teaching.pdf

OECD. (2009). Creating effective teaching and learning environments. First results from TALIS. Retrieved 27 June, 2015, from www.oecd.org/edu/school/43023606.pdf

Shanahan, T. and Shanahan, C. (2012). What is disciplinary literacy and why does it matter? *Top Language Disorders*, 31(1), 7–18. DOI: 10.1097/TLD.0b013e318244557a

# Index

Note: 'N' after a page number indicates a note; 'f' indicates a figure; 't' indicates a table.